JUMP START COFFEESCRIPT

BY EARLE CASTLEDINE

Jump Start CoffeeScript

by Earle Castledine

Copyright © 2012 SitePoint Pty. Ltd.

Product Manager: Simon Mackie   **Expert Reviewer**: Craig Sharkie

Technical Editor: Diana MacDonald   **English Editor**: Kelly Steele

Assistant Technical Editor: Ben Axnick   **Cover Designer**: Alex Walker

Indexer: Glenda Browne

Notice of Rights

Notice of Liability

Trademark Notice

Published by SitePoint Pty. Ltd.

48 Cambridge Street Collingwood
VIC Australia 3066
Web: www.sitepoint.com
Email: business@sitepoint.com

ISBN 978-0-9872478-2-7 (print)

ISBN 978-0-9872478-3-4 (ebook)
Printed and bound in the United States of America

Dedication

To Amelia: If I could write, I'd write a book for you.

About the Author

Sporting a Masters in Information Technology and a lifetime of experience on the Web of Hard Knocks, Earle Castledine (aka Mr Speaker) holds an interest in everything computery. Raised in the wild by various 8-bit home computers, he settled in the Internet during the mid-nineties and has been living and working there ever since.

A senior systems analyst and JavaScript flâneur, he is equally happy in the muddy pits of .NET code, the dense foliage of mobile apps and games, and the fluffy clouds of client-side interaction development.

As co-creator of client-side opus http://www.turntubelist.com/, as well as many web-based experiments, Earle recognizes the Internet not as a lubricant for social change, but as a vehicle for unleashing frivolous ECMAScript gadgets and interesting time-wasting technologies.

About the Expert Reviewer

Craig was once happy to call himself a developer, speaker, author, and advocate. Since then, he's added JS meet founder and JSConf organizer to the list—and expert reviewer. Should you add husband and father, and you'd be getting closer to working out why he's often unreasonably happy. In 2000, he was asked by short-sighted bosses where he wanted to be in five years' time, and twelve years on he's still doing the same thing—working with languages he loves in a community that expands on possibilities as fast as it creates them.

About SitePoint

SitePoint specializes in publishing fun, practical, and easy-to-understand content for web professionals. Visit http://www.sitepoint.com/ to access our blogs, books, newsletters, articles, and community forums. You'll find a stack of information on JavaScript, PHP, Ruby, Mobile, design, and more.

About Jump Start

Jump Start books provide you with a rapid and practical introduction to web development languages and technologies. Around 150 pages in length, they can be read in a weekend, giving you a solid grounding in the topic and the confidence to experiment on your own.

Table of Contents

Preface

CoffeeScript is "a little language that compiles into JavaScript."[1] It aims to smooth over some of JavaScript's rougher edges while highlighting and augmenting the impressive flexibility at the core of the JavaScript language. It's clean, concise, and maintainable, and makes writing client-side code really, *really* fun.

Jump Start CoffeeScript is a book about CoffeeScript. Its goal is to help you become productive with CoffeeScript as quickly as possible. From the first line in the book, you'll be writing code that shows just how easy it is to take the plunge into this delightfully addictive world.

Along the way, we'll make a game. Not just the outer husk of a boring space-based shoot 'em up, but a complete, extensible HTML5 game with tile maps, particle effects, AI, and (of course) ninjas. You'll see how CoffeeScript's succinctness and elegance is the perfect partner for effectively prototyping and refining your ideas.

That's it. By the end of this book, you'll know how to make HTML5 games, and proficiently code (and think) in CoffeeScript, as well as have a deeper understanding of the power and beauty of JavaScript itself.

Who Should Read This Book

If you have some knowledge of web programming concepts and want to streamline writing JavaScript, this book is for you.

Conventions Used

You'll notice that we've used certain typographic and layout styles throughout this book to signify different types of information. Look out for the following items.

Code Samples

Code in this book will be displayed using a fixed-width font, like so:

---

[1] http://coffeescript.org/

```
<h1>A Perfect Summer's Day</h1>
<p>It was a lovely day for a walk in the park. The birds
were singing and the kids were all back at school.</p>
```

If the code is to be found in the book's code archive, the name of the file will appear at the top of the program listing, like this:

example.css

```
.footer {
  background-color: #CCC;
  border-top: 1px solid #333;
}
```

If only part of the file is displayed, this is indicated by the word *excerpt*:

example.css *(excerpt)*

```
  border-top: 1px solid #333;
```

If additional code is to be inserted into an existing example, the new code will be displayed in bold:

```
function animate() {
  new_variable = "Hello";
}
```

Also, where existing code is required for context, rather than repeat all the code, a ⋮ will be displayed:

```
function animate() {
  ⋮
  return new_variable;
}
```

Some lines of code are intended to be entered on one line, but we've had to wrap them because of page constraints. A ➡ indicates a line break that exists for formatting purposes only, and should be ignored.

```
URL.open("http://jspro.com/raw-javascript/how-to-create-custom-even
➥ts-in-javascript/");
```

Tips, Notes, and Warnings

Hey, You!

Tips will give you helpful little pointers.

Ahem, Excuse Me …

Notes are useful asides that are related—but not critical—to the topic at hand.
Think of them as extra tidbits of information.

Make Sure You Always …

… pay attention to these important points.

Watch Out!

Warnings will highlight any gotchas that are likely to trip you up along the way.

Supplementary Materials

http://www.sitepoint.com/books/coffeescript1/
The book's website, containing links, updates, resources, and more.

http://www.sitepoint.com/books/coffeescript1/code.php
The downloadable code archive for this book.

http://www.sitepoint.com/forums/forumdisplay.php?15-JavaScript-amp-jQuery
SitePoint's JavaScript forum, for help on any tricky CoffeeScript problems.

books@sitepoint.com
Our email address, should you need to contact us for support, to report a problem, or for any other reason.

Challenge Yourself

Once you've mastered CoffeeScript, test yourself with our online quiz. With questions based on the book's content, only true CoffeeScript champions can achieve a perfect score. Head on over to http://quizpoint.com/#categories/COFFEESCRIPT.

Friends of SitePoint

Thanks for buying this book. We really appreciate your support! We now think of you as a "Friend of SitePoint," and so would like to invite you to our special "Friends of SitePoint" page.[2] Here you can SAVE up to 43% on a range of other super-cool SitePoint products, just by using the password: `friends`.

[2] http://sitepoint.com/friends

Getting Started

CoffeeScript is a programming language that looks like this:

```
hello = (name) ->
  alert "Hello, #{name}!"

hello "World"
```

Here, we're defining and then calling a function, `hello`, which accepts a single parameter, `name`, and is displayed in an annoying fashion on the screen (via `alert`). If you're a coder, you've probably identified a few interesting elements in this piece of code. Indeed, one of this book's goals is to thoroughly explore the syntactic and pragmatic choices that make CoffeeScript an interesting programming language.

CoffeeScript occupies a weird space in the programming language landscape: it was designed from the beginning to piggyback on top of JavaScript, the de facto language of the Web. CoffeeScript code is transpiled (or transcompiled) directly into JavaScript code, a cunning trick to leverage the ubiquity of the web browser as an execution environment. This means that CoffeeScript runs wherever JavaScript runs, and can do whatever JavaScript can do. And with the rise of technologies like Node.js and HTML5, that's a lot of places and a lot of functionality.

Why write a language that's simply a copy of another language? Because the primary purpose of CoffeeScript is to be a simpler version of JavaScript. CoffeeScript aims to highlight and streamline the fantastically powerful parts of its progenitor while concealing and repairing its rough spots. It aims to be more expressive, yet more succinct. It aims to be fun.

How? Without going into details (and never mind if some of the following sounds like gibberish), CoffeeScript provides us with a bunch of features that we currently lack: nicer syntax, function binding (to help with scoping issues), multiline strings, splats (for neatly handling variable parameter lengths), lambda functions with implicit returns, list comprehensions, destructuring, ranges, simple classes with inheritance, string interpolation, a funky existential operator ... and so much more.

A side effect of learning CoffeeScript is that you will improve at JavaScript. If you're here because you hate JavaScript and never want to see another line of it, I have bad news: CoffeeScript is not an attempt to kill JavaScript (unlike some newer transpiled languages—I'm looking at you, Dart), but to co-exist and ultimately help improve JavaScript itself. That's how good it is!

HTML5 Game Jam Challenge

It's 9.00 a.m. on Monday morning. You're sitting in a coffee shop, eagerly awaiting the arrival of your fellow team members to commence your entry in the "7-day HTML5 Game Jam-a-Thon Challenge (TM)," as advertised in Figure 1.1. The rules are simple: You have seven days to create an HTML5 video game from scratch.

Figure 1.1. Game Jam-a-Thon

Our game will be a traditional 2D platform-type affair, with bad guys and platforms and ladders and such—and you've decided that it's the perfect project to learn some CoffeeScript. Of course, you've failed to mention to your teammates that, despite the incredibly tight time frame for the competition, you're going to write the game in a language that you have no experience in. We'd better take a few minutes to learn some of the basics before they arrive …

The Basics

First up, how can we run some code? It turns out that the options available for executing CoffeeScript are legion. As we only have a few minutes to get up to speed, we'll choose the simplest:

- Head to the CoffeeScript website [http://www.coffeescript.org].
- Select the **Try CoffeeScript** tab.
- Activate the **Run** button, as shown in Figure 1.2.

Figure 1.2. Hello CoffeeScript

Ebbs and Flows

The Internet ebbs and flows like the tides, and by the time you read this text, the "click-to-run" functionality may have moved, morphed, or disappeared from the CoffeeScript website. If that's the case, don't fear: we're covering more options in the section called "Starting the Game Project".

The default code is a simple alert box that shows the text, "Hello, CoffeeScript!" Any CoffeeScript code in the left panel will be transpiled to its JavaScript output, shown in the right-hand panel, and executed. The actual pop-up box implementation is not from CoffeeScript, but from the native browser code that's called from the JavaScript output. When we're using CoffeeScript in the browser, we have access to the DOM as we do in JavaScript.

Let's remove the default CoffeeScript code and add some of our own. We'll create a small function to reverse a string. There's no need to fully understand it yet (try to figure it out, though!), but if you're typing along at home, you might want to indent using spaces because hitting **tab** will change the focused area:

```coffeescript
# Simple string reversal function
reverse = (sentence) ->
  sentence
    .split("")
    .reverse()
    .join("")

# Now use our new reversing powers!
text = "rats live on"
backwards = reverse text
alert "#{text} #{backwards}"
```

Running this will reward you with a popup containing the forward and reversed text.

Running Directly in the Browser

How is our code—which isn't JavaScript—running directly in the browser like this? Perhaps you'd guess it's sending it off to the server for compilation? Nope. The trick is, *CoffeeScript is written in CoffeeScript*. And, as you know, CoffeeScript outputs to JavaScript. Therefore, the CoffeeScript compiler can be included in a web page and compiled on the fly.

Let's contrast that block of code with how we'd write it using plain JavaScript:

```javascript
var text, backwards;

// Simple string reversal function
function reverse(sentence) {
  return sentence
    .split("")
    .reverse()
    .join("");
}

// Now use our new reversing powers!
```

```
text = "rats live on";
backwards = reverse(text);
alert(text + " " + backwards);
```

You'll probably notice that the CoffeeScript and JavaScript versions are fairly similar. That's not surprising in this case because we're using only a few of CoffeeScript's fancy features, and the guts of the algorithm (the split/reverse/join manipulation) is simply using JavaScript's native methods. The truth is—especially when you're beginning—you can mostly get away with writing CoffeeScript just like JavaScript. So it's easy to begin writing code and add in the cool tricks as you learn them.

Here's some more simple CoffeeScript and its corresponding JavaScript output. Nothing will happen when you run this (because collided is never true); it's merely to highlight more differences. If you're just starting out with CoffeeScript, comparing the before and after code is *invaluable* for learning how it works:

```
lives = 3
collided = false

# ...after some game logic...

if collided
  lives = lives - 1
  alert "Game Over" if lives is 0
```

Once compiled, this will spit out the following:

```
var collided, lives;

lives = 3;
collided = false;

if (collided) {
  lives = lives - 1;
  if (lives === 0) {
    alert("Game Over");
  }
}
```

> ### JavaScript under the Hood
>
> This is the actual JavaScript that the CoffeeScript transpiles itself into. It may not be exactly how you'd write your own JavaScript, but it is functionally equivalent.

In CoffeeScript, we don't use a `var` declaration; it's done for us, and we're using some kind of weird inverted syntax to test `if lives is 0`. Even in these two brief snippets, there are a bunch of small and important differences between the languages. I'm warning you now: if you're a long-time JavaScripter, some of them might rub you the wrong way at first, so hang tight …

Missing Cruft

CoffeeScript does away with a bundle of the boilerplate elements of JavaScript code: semicolons and curly braces are gone, there are no `var` keywords for variable definitions, parentheses are often omitted when calling functions, and function and return statements are nowhere to be seen.

This is a considered attempt on CoffeeScript's part to remove as much as possible that's not directly related to the problem you're trying to solve. For those of us who have spent our whole lives with the function/return construct, it seems a minor point; like people who swear they don't even notice advertisements anymore, we're sure that the cruft has no effect on us. But just as with advertising, the cruft is still there, doing its best to be confused with content—making it harder to parse (visually), and easier for bugs to stay hidden.

A pleasant side effect of this cruft removal is that CoffeeScript programs are noticeably shorter than their JavaScript counterparts.

Whitespace

Superficially, JavaScript looks a lot like C or Java—that's why we have curly braces to delimit code blocks. CoffeeScript decided to go the Ruby/Python route and use **significant whitespace**—tabs and spaces—to define a statement block. Nested blocks are achieved by nesting indentation levels. Be sure to keep indentation consistent within each source file (and for your sanity, across the entire project!). So if you're using two spaces, always use two spaces; otherwise, the compiler can become lost.

Historically, programmers will fervently fight for or against "spaces or braces" in the same way they'd argue "tabs versus spaces." CoffeeScript avoids some of the problems of significant whitespace by virtue of its transpiled nature; for example, people dislike that whitespace is unable to be minimized, unlike curly-brace programming languages. However, as our output is JavaScript, it's this output that will be the target of our minimization efforts.

Comments

Comments aren't executed:

```
# Commencing a line with a # indicates a comment
```

What's more, they're excluded from the JavaScript output:

So, this is a case where CoffeeScript is, in fact, more verbose than JavaScript! If you want a multiline comment block, you use the triple hashes:

```
###
  Everything you put here will be ignored. Unlike
  single-line comments - these show up in the output.
###
```

This will produce the following:

```
/*
  Everything you put here will be ignored. Unlike
  single-line comments - these show up in the output.
*/
```

Multiline comments are included in the compiled output; this makes them useful for adding block headers to each file, for example.

Types, Variables, and Scope

CoffeeScript types are JavaScript types: numbers are numbers, strings are strings, Booleans are Booleans. But the way variables are handled is quite different. As you've seen from the examples so far, there is no var statement in CoffeeScript—it's handled automatically. So, if you had the following variable declarations in JavaScript:

```
var result = [],
    count = 0,
    $el;
```

… the equivalent in CoffeeScript would be simply:

```
result = []
count = 0
```

We wouldn't define `$el` because we're yet to use it! When you define a variable in CoffeeScript, the `var` declaration is pushed up to the closest scope that the variable is in (similar to Ruby's local scope). This avoids the common pitfall in JavaScript of accidentally creating global variables—though it does mean you need to take care to avoid reusing variable names when you nest functions, because the inner variable will just be a reference to the outer variable.

CoffeeScript also helps out with some of the other fun parts of JavaScript scope, which we'll delve into later.

Functions

Functions are one of the most powerful aspects of JavaScript. They are first-class citizens of the language, because you can pass a function as a parameter or return a function as the result from another function. You can compose them—just as you can in other functional programming languages, such as Lisp. In fact, as JavaScript's resident guru, Douglas Crockford, once said, JavaScript has more in common with functional languages like Lisp or Scheme than with C or Java.[1]

You might not be sold on functional programming (*cough* just yet *cough*), but it's a paradigm that is very powerful and a lot of fun. As an example, part of jQuery's success is due to the joy of being able to chain a bunch of functions together to manipulate and process lists of DOM nodes. Each step of the jQuery chain returns a new list, and the lists can be filtered or transformed as needed.

---

[1] http://javascript.crockford.com/javascript

If you utilize a functional style—or do a lot of asynchronous work—you would have noticed an issue with JavaScript: a large chunk of your code consists of the `function` and `return` keywords. Consider the following JavaScript snippet that takes an array of angles in degrees, converts them to radians, and then returns only values that appear in the first two quadrants (the "top half" of the circle), as seen in Figure 1.3.

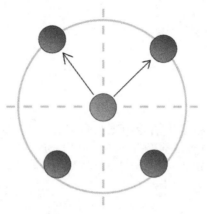

Figure 1.3. Danger ahead

We might do this in a game to fetch directions to enemies in our field of view:

```javascript
[45, 135, 225, 315].map(function(degrees) {
  return degrees * (Math.PI / 180);
}).filter(function(radians) {
  return radians % (2 * Math.PI) < Math.PI;
});
```

First we use `map` to convert degrees to radians, then `filter` to only keep the values we're interested in. Here's the same code in CoffeeScript (please note that there are more idiomatic ways to do mapping and filtering in CoffeeScript, but this is just to highlight the difference between function declarations):

```coffeescript
[45, 135, 225, 315].map (degrees) ->
    degrees * (Math.PI / 180)
  .filter (radians) ->
    radians % (2 * Math.PI) < Math.PI
```

Even for this tiny (albeit convoluted) demonstration, that's 158 JavaScript bytes versus 128 CoffeeScript bytes. Again, typing a few extra characters is not the issue; the point is that our CoffeeScript code contains just the bare essentials to define our problem. In this case, it does it by replacing the `function` keyword with the symbol `->`, and by having **implicit returns**.

The CoffeeScript compiler tries to make sure that all statements in the language can be used as expressions, so nearly everything will have a return value. The last expression inside a function will give the value that's returned. Consider:

```
square = (x) -> x * x
```

 Short Syntax

This short function syntax is out-and-out a good idea; so good that it's been accepted into the next version of JavaScript. I'm trusting that by the time you read this book, it will be part of the standard and already implemented in your browser—and this whole section will seem obvious to you. If that's the case, just remember: you have CoffeeScript to thank for it!

Starting the Game Project

Hmmm, this is a bad sign. It's the kick-off meeting on day one and your team is already half an hour late. After ordering another cup of coffee,[2] you decide you might as well start on the game. The first step is to create the base project and set up your environment for development.

Installing: an Overview

As we mentioned right at the beginning, CoffeeScript sits in a bit of a weird space for a language. For most programming languages, "installing" means downloading a package from the author's website and running it. But CoffeeScript is a bit different: the core compiler is available as a command line tool that can be run in any JavaScript environment, and at the present time this means running under Node.js.

Node.js is a popular platform for running JavaScript applications. It's often used as a web server for serving apps that use JavaScript as both the client- and server-side language. However, CoffeeScript uses it for running its command line tool that compiles our sources. We need to install both Node.js and then the `coffee` tool.

---

[2] Please note, this is not a coffee pun. We've strived to eliminate all coffee-based puns from the book.

Client-side Compilation on the Fly

"My teammates will be here *any minute*, and you expect me to install and configure the whole internet in ten seconds? There must be another way ... ," you grumble to yourself. Well, there is another way. But you have to *promise* after you have tried it and written some code to read the next section on installing things properly.

On the CoffeeScript.org website, we were running code and executing it live. This worked because CoffeeScript is written in CoffeeScript, so the compiler itself can be output as plain-old JavaScript. You can download a special version of this JavaScript that, when included in your web page, automatically compiles any CoffeeScript code snippets on the page. Magic!

Not for General Consumption

This technique of finding and compiling pieces of CoffeeScript in the page is a novel and interesting idea, but it's inefficient. Every page view requires the compiler to be loaded unnecessarily (it should be cached after the first view), and every chunk of code must be recompiled—which, depending on the complexity and size of the code, can be very slow. It's a useful tool for testing, but if you're serving pages to the grand public, you should be using precompiled JavaScript.

The first step is to grab the compiler. The official source repository for the entire project is on Jeremy Ashkenas's (the creator of CoffeeScript—commit that name to memory!) GitHub repository at https://github.com/jashkenas/coffee-script. At the moment, we're only interested in the JavaScript file for the browser. This lives in the **extras/** directory of the repository, or you can grab it from the direct link via the website at http://coffeescript.org/extras/coffee-script.js.

Save the file to your project—wherever you'd normally put your third-party scripts (I'm putting it in the **/vendor** directory)—and include it in the page:

chapter01/01jsandcs/index.html *(excerpt)*

```
<script src="vendor/coffee-script.js"></script>
```

To define a snippet of CoffeeScript, you have to wrap it in a `script` tag and give it the custom `type` `text/coffeescript` (rather than the usual `text/javascript`). This prevents the browser from trying to execute it as regular JavaScript, and gives the CoffeeScript library a way to find all the code it needs to compile:

```
<script type="text/coffeescript">
  alert "Look ma! no braces!"
</script>
```

These snippets can be sprinkled anywhere in the code, though you should probably follow good practices and place your scripts at the bottom of the page. Here's a full example, including both our favorite languages together:

chapter01/01jsandcs/index.html

```
<!DOCTYPE html>
<html>
<head>
  <meta charset="utf-8">
  <title>HTML5 Game Jam Entry</title>
</head>
<body>
  <h1>Ready to RUMBLE!</h1>
  <script src="vendor/coffee-script.js"
    type="text/javascript"></script>

  <!-- Run some JavaScript -->
  <script type="text/javascript">
    alert("JavaScript is here.");
  </script>

  <!-- Run some CoffeeScript -->
  <script type="text/coffeescript">
    alert "CoffeeScript is here, too!"
  </script>
</body>
</html>
```

CoffeeScript running directly in the browser ... weird! If you didn't get the alert dialog, double-check the path to the library, and be sure you set the script type correctly. You should make sure the functions we wrote above work here too.

Installing CoffeeScript Properly

It's time to get serious. Our real goal setup is to create an environment that lets us run the `coffee` utility, which is a command-line tool for turning CoffeeScript files into JavaScript files that we then include in our web pages like any ordinary resource.

No Installation Required

Some web frameworks such as Ruby on Rails[3] and the Play! framework[4] support CoffeeScript by default. If you're using such a framework, none of this installation is necessary; just place your **.coffee** files in the correct place and the framework will compile them for you. If CoffeeScript is not supported by your framework of choice, write the creators a persuasive email today!

Installing Node.js

First up, you'll need the latest stable version of the Node.js platform. Handy installers are available for Windows and Mac from the download page at http://nodejs.org/download/. If you're in a Unix environment, you can also grab the sources from the download page or install via your distro's package manager.[5]

Once the install is complete, you should be able to run Node.js from your terminal via `node`, as shown in Figure 1.4. If the install completed correctly but the node command was not found, be sure to restart your shell session, and check that the Node path exists in your shell environment path.

---

[3] http://www.rubyonrails.org
[4] http://www.playframework.org
[5] https://github.com/joyent/node/wiki/Installing-Node.js-via-package-manager

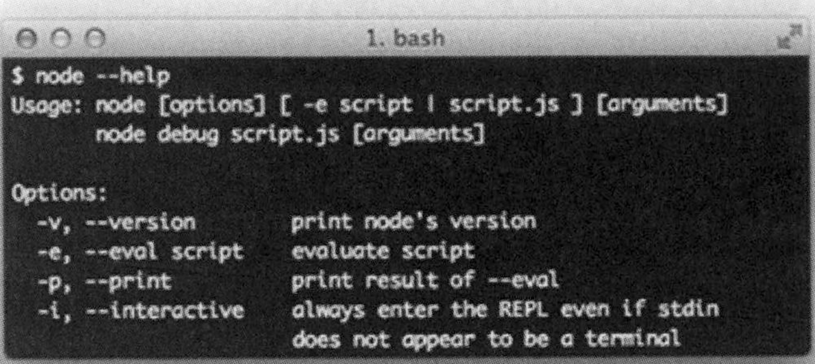

Figure 1.4. Running Node.js from your terminal

Installing Coffee

The next step is to install `coffee`. The easiest way to do this is via npm, Node's package manager for installing modules. This is installed when you install Node, so it should already be available to you. Try it out with the following command (if you're still on the Node command line, you'll need to exit by pressing **Ctrl-d**):

```
npm --version
```

We want to use npm to grab the `coffee-script` module[6] (note the hyphen). To actually install the module, use npm's `install` command:

```
npm install -g coffee-script
```

Global versus Local

On the official Node.js blog, sparing use of global installs is recommended.[7] The guideline is to use a global install if the package needs to be accessed on the command line, as in our case.

This will fetch the module and make it available via Node.js. You can make sure everything has gone to plan by opening up a new console session and asking for some help on our new module:

---

[6] https://npmjs.org/package/coffee-script
[7] http://blog.nodejs.org/2011/03/23/npm-1-0-global-vs-local-installation/

```
coffee --help
```

This should show output in the vein of Figure 1.5.

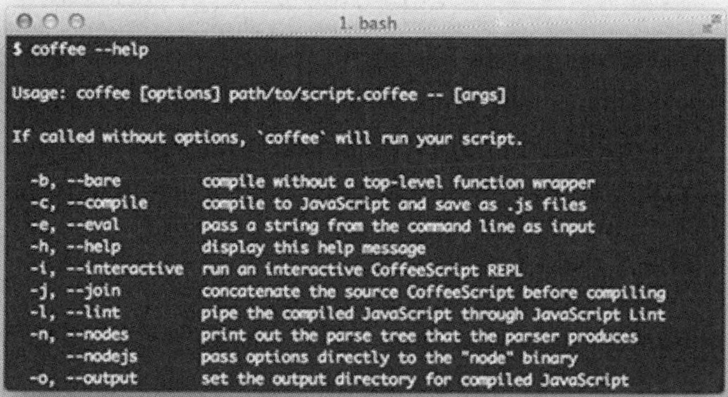

Figure 1.5. Outputting CoffeeScript help

Coffee Options

That's it for installing—our system is now fully operational. The last step is to figure out how to integrate `coffee` into our workflow. By default, the `coffee` utility will run .**coffee** files. To test it out, create a blank document in your text editor and save it as **friday.coffee**; then add the following:

chapter01/02isitfriday/script.coffee *(excerpt)*

```
day = new Date().getDay()
isFriday = if day == 5 then "YES!" else "no."

console.log "Is it Friday? #{isFriday}"
```

Finally, a tool to tell us if it's Friday or not! Again, don't worry too much about the syntax for now, but the final line is used to log to the screen output (because an alert is only for the browser). To run it, type the following at your prompt (making sure you are in the same directory as the file):

```
coffee friday.coffee
```

The output, of course, will depend on the day you run it! Now we know how to make command line tools, but that's no good for an HTML5 game—we need JavaScript files. First, modify the `console.log` to be an alert (we'll look more at `console.log` in the section called "`alert` versus `console.log`" in Chapter 2):

chapter01/02isitfriday/script.coffee *(excerpt)*

```
alert "Is it Friday? #{isFriday}"
```

Now it's time to compile the CoffeeScript code using the `--compile` (or `-c`) flag:

```
coffee -c script.coffee
```

This generates a JavaScript file of the same name in the same directory, but with the **.js** extension. Open up this file now and have a look at what `coffee` has done. It's plain ol' JavaScript, which we can link to in a website as usual:

chapter01/02isitfriday/index.html *(excerpt)*

```
<!DOCTYPE html>
<html>
<head>
  <title>Is it Friday?</title>
</head>
<body>
  <script src="script.js" type="text/javascript"></script>
</body>
</html>
```

The `coffee` tool has a stack of features that we'll use as we go along. At the moment, you'll notice that every time you make a change in your **.coffee** source file, you need to rerun the `coffee` command. We'll look at how to bypass this, and create an efficient coding workflow in Chapter 2.

Choosing Our Tech

We've come so far, but still only have an alert dialog to show for our efforts. It's time to make some executive decisions on how this game is going to work, and put some action up on the screen.

Document Object Model

We have a few options when it comes to rendering HTML5 games. The oldest and most widely supported is to use positioned DOM elements, such as `divs` or DOM images. Elements will be dynamically added and removed from the container with their appropriate animation frame or tile image. During the render phase of our game loop, we update the `style` properties of elements that have changed. For example, we might update a player's DOM element (`el`) in response to a player model:

```
el.style.left = player.x
el.style.top = player.y
```

There are a few advantages of using the DOM. Being inherent to a web page, it's the most "web" of all our options; like any regular DOM element, you can easily attach mouse event handlers—like `mouseover` or `mousedown`—to individual elements of your game (you have to calculate this manually otherwise). You can also right-click on your player and see debug information with your regular debugging tools.

The DOM is supported absolutely everywhere on the Web (albeit with the familiar cross-browser problems that you have to deal with in web development). There's also a lot of work being done by the browser vendors on hardware acceleration of the DOM, so rendering games can be as fast as—or faster than—a canvas equivalent.

The disadvantages are that the browser can quickly slow down if your game contains a lot of entities that are onscreen at the same time. Anytime a node in a web page is changed, the browser is forced to perform a reflow, updating and repainting everything. This is generally the slowest operation the browser performs. There are ways to minimize this issue (using document fragments that are replaced in bulk)—but if you're trying to make Raiden IV,[8] you're going to notice slowdowns.

Finally, the biggest disadvantage to using the DOM is that you're limited in your graphical processing abilities. You have no access to the individual pixels on the screen, so all your effects—such as explosions or particle effects—can only be done with static images, rather than be generated programmatically.

---

[8] http://en.wikipedia.org/wiki/Raiden_(video_game)

Canvas

To circumvent this limitation, HTML5 has given us the `canvas` element. This is a block-level element that consumes a rectangular space in your web page, like an image—except it's a visual that we can alter with JavaScript! The Canvas API has many cool features: drawing and compositing shapes and paths, manipulating and transforming images, filling with gradients, and setting individual pixels. You can see some of them in action in Figure 1.6.

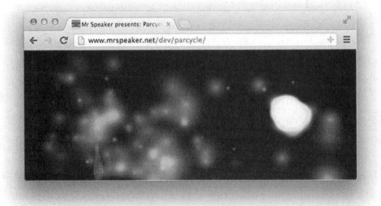

Figure 1.6. A particle effect system running completely in canvas

Support for canvas is growing, and the browser implementations are constantly improving (which means canvas animations will run faster). The API is quite simple, but lets us do an impressive number of graphical operations—certainly enough for turning out some fantastic-looking games.

However, rendering to canvas is very different to the DOM. Our processing flexibility comes at a price: we have to manually draw everything in the correct position for every frame. With the DOM, we can use CSS transitions to say "move the player from here to there over a ten-second period." With canvas, we have to take care of all that ourselves. Additionally, if we want to know if the user clicked on a button in our game, we have to take the x and y coordinates of the mouse and figure out if there's a button at that position (at least, until hit regions are widely supported)!

Further Options

Although many HTML games use either DOM or canvas for rendering, there are a few more options available to us. SVG (Scalable Vector Graphics) is widely supported, is fantastic for drawing and manipulating vector graphics, and lets you easily add event handlers to nodes. It's less commonly used for games at the moment, but if you want your graphics to scale to different devices easily, it's worth a look!

And if two dimensions are just not enough, WebGL is the new kid in town. It brings the raw power of OpenGL to the browser, opening the door for very advanced 3D games. Learning OpenGL is a whole world of pain, however, so we're not even going to consider it at the moment. If we were, it would definitely be via the awesome three.js library,[9] which simplifies building 3D games significantly, as shown by the graphics in Figure 1.7.

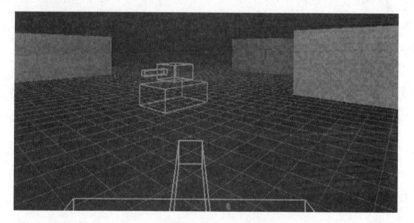

Figure 1.7. Three.js 3D tank game

When generating games, it's good practice to separate the game logic from the rendering code; then, at runtime, you can choose which render to use. So if the browser has no support for canvas, you can render to the DOM or use SVG. If you want to be extremely crazy, you could even create a version that renders to the 16×16 pixel browser favicon like the classic "Defender of the Favicon"![10]

---

[9] http://mrdoob.github.com/three.js/
[10] http://www.p01.org/releases/DEFENDER_of_the_favicon/

Drawing Something: Using Canvas

Alas, we only have seven days to create this game, so we're going to keep development simple (yet powerful!) and use the Canvas API for rendering our game. The ultimate goal will be to import our graphics as sprite sheets for making animations and so forth. But first of all, it's time to push some pixels on the screen. Plop a `canvas` element into your web page using a unique ID:

chapter01/03disco/index.html *(excerpt)*

```html
<canvas id="game"></canvas>
```

Now we need to grab a reference to its drawing context via CoffeeScript:

chapter01/03disco/script.coffee *(excerpt)*

```coffee
ctx = document
  .getElementById("game")
  .getContext("2d")

ctx.fillStyle = "#000"
ctx.fillRect 0, 0, ctx.canvas.width, ctx.canvas.height
```

 Compile Your File

If you're compiling this code with `coffee`, it needs to be in a separate file, compiled, then included in the web page. See **chapter01/03disco/** for the full code.

There you go, a black rectangle. Any canvas drawing operations need to be done against a context that we fetch by calling the `getContext("2d")` method on the `canvas` DOM element. When we implement this for our actual game, we'll have to add in a check that the user's browser actually does support the `canvas` element; for now, we'll let it slide.

Once you have a canvas context, we can use all of its API methods to draw awesome visuals on the screen. So far, we've only set the `fillStyle` (this can be a named color, or a hex, RGB(A), or HSL(A) value; note, however, support for CSS3 color notation varies across browsers) and filled a solid rectangle to the screen (starting at coordinate 0, 0 from the top-left corner and using the canvas's `width` and `height` to know its size) with `fillRect`.

So we have an object on the screen, but it's hardly exciting. Let's jump ahead a little in our CoffeeScript studies for the purpose of spicing it up a bit. Underneath the `fillRect` command, add in the following code:

chapter01/03disco/script.coffee *(excerpt)*

```
noise = ->
  for x in [0..20]
    for y in [0..10]
      color = Math.floor(Math.random() * 360)
      ctx.fillStyle = "hsl(#{color}, 60%, 50%)"
      ctx.fillRect x * 15, y * 15, 14, 14

setInterval noise, 100
```

This will produce the image shown in Figure 1.8.

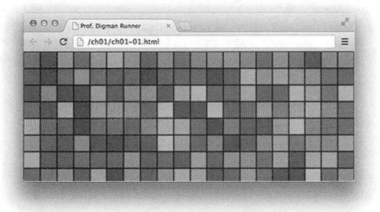

Figure 1.8. 1970s disco squares

Form, movement, color … it's seventies disco time! Movement is indicated in the last line: the `setInterval` call. This is a standard JavaScript method that executes a given function repeatedly at a given interval time (in our code, that's every 100 milliseconds). We ask it to call our `noise` function.

Unlike the "hello world" function typed at the very start of this chapter, `noise` takes no parameters, so there's no need to add empty parentheses in the definition. The next couple of lines might look a bit odd; they're responsible for creating the grid that the li'l rectangles snap to (we'll dissect them fully in the section called "Loops and Ranges" in Chapter 2).

Finally, the meat of the routine: drawing hundreds of little squares. First, we choose a random color hue; then fill a 14×14 pixel rectangle at every grid position. The grid position is determined by multiplying the x and y coordinates by 15. Because the grid is 15 pixels, and we only draw rectangles 14 pixels squared, there is a one-pixel black line separating them. This is just the background showing through.

HSL Colors

Choosing some nice-looking random colors with a very small amount of code can be tough. The trick we've used here is to take advantage of `canvas`'s support or HSL (Hue/Saturation/Lightness) colors. HSL is an alternative to the RGB and hex (#00000-style) color definitions. In HSL, the first value represents the hue in a range: 0 (and 360) is red, 120 is green, and 240 is blue. Other numbers are hues in between them. The second parameter is the saturation, and the last is the lightness. These parameters are defined as percentages.

To generate our assortment of colors with HSL, we just select a random shade between 0 and 360, turn the saturation and lightness down a bit, and voilà—nice random colors!

We're on Our Way

"Oooh, what's that?" asks your pixel artist over your shoulder. They're an hour and a half late, but finally the team has sheepishly wandered into the café. It comprises a pixel artist, a web designer, and a story writer/ideas person—plus you, the coder.

"Where have you folk been?" you ask. They look at you blankly. You give them a rundown of your progress so far, and how the game will be written in CoffeeScript using canvas. You point at the colorful squares flashing on your screen and they nod with vague comprehension. You explain that the game will be a 2D platformer with retro-style graphics and some nice effects—unless they have any other ideas? They stare blankly again.

Looks like you'll be taking the lead on this project. Thankfully, CoffeeScript is well-positioned to help you in your mission. And we've only just scratched the surface of its flexibility and power!

CoffeeScript Fundamentals

It's Day 2 of the inaugural "7-day HTML5 Game Jam-a-Thon Challenge (TM)," and the situation has gone from bad to worse. After last night's team kick-off party, everyone else decided to go out on the town for "one more." It's now 11.00 a.m. and still no sign of any team members. Your questions about graphic concepts and plot suggestions remain unanswered in your outbox, and you're bored with waiting.

Lacking real direction on where the game is headed, we might have to set our own goals for the day. First up, we need to learn enough CoffeeScript to be able to code *anything*. There may be a cleaner and more efficient way to code our solutions, but we want to be able to solve any problem that comes our way. If we're successful, we can feel more comfortable about finishing our game in time (and we can convince our manager to let us use CoffeeScript for the mega-corporate client project they just won).

Our secondary goal is to apply our newfound knowledge to the task of properly bootstrapping our game, and putting some real assets on the screen: a title screen, or some characters and backgrounds. That's a lot to do ... so let's get cracking!

More of the Basics

Like any language, it's going to take us a while before we become proficient. It's impossible to master everything right away, but we have a tight schedule, so we need to be productive, fast! Because we're looking at the very basics, we'll have to first work through some examples that aren't *directly* related to the creation of our game. But never fear, we'll only spend a short time in boring-example land before delving into the exciting world of our game.

Setting Up Our Project

Our initial project tree will look like Figure 2.1. The details are sketchy, and you probably have your own idea of where everything should go, but it'll do for a base.

Figure 2.1. Planning our project tree

As you can see, it's just a basic web structure. The most important parts are the **src** and **scripts** folders. The **src** folder will hold all our **.coffee** files for the entire game. These are compiled directly into the **script** folder, from where they can be imported into our **index.html** page.

Let's open up our editor, and add a message to the **game.coffee** file:

chapter02/src/game.coffee

```
alert "Game loaded!"
```

There are many ways to compile files for CoffeeScript. For smaller projects, the method described below will suffice. For larger projects, refer to the section called "Building Larger Projects" in Chapter 3. In the last chapter, we compiled individual input files to matching output files. The `coffee` tool can also combine all the scripts into one script, so we only have one HTTP request to load in our **index.html** file.

Another indispensable feature is `coffee`'s ability to watch a directory for changes. This means anytime you make a change in a source file, the code is compiled and deployed instantly. The command we'll be using to join and watch our game files looks like this (and assumes it is being run from the **src/** directory):

```
coffee -j ../script/main.js -w -c game.coffee
```

This will populate the **script** folder with the **main.js** file. Now we can include this in our web page:

```
                                                                    chapter02/index.html

<!DOCTYPE html>
<html>
  <head>
    <meta charset=UTF-8>
    <link rel="stylesheet" href="css/main.css">
  </head>
  <body>
    <div id="container">
      <canvas id="game" width="580" height="480"></canvas>
    </div>
    <script src="script/main.js" type="text/javascript"></script>
  </body>
</html>
```

Loading the page should give us the console message, and changing the **.coffee** file and refreshing the page should update it. Note that the page includes a reference to a CSS file to improve the game's appearance by automatically tiling the background image. If you wish to use it, the file is available at **chapter02/css/main.css**. With that said, we're now ready to code!

`alert` versus `console.log`

Before we move on, let's look at our alternatives to testing via `alert`. So far, we've been `alert`ing things to see some output. It's a tried-and-true method of debugging code, but we have some better choices at our disposal these days. Modern versions of Chrome and Firefox—along with IE9—contain a `console` tool for this purpose so that our debugging avoids blocking the main browser thread as it does with the `alert` dialog. The APIs differ from browser to browser—and browser extensions can expand on this (some support amazing debugging features, so be sure to check out what your browser offers[1])—but generally they'll support at least a couple of standard methods:

```
console.log "No more alerts!"
console.error "In case something goes wrong."
```

These will appear in the console window, which can be opened from a keyboard shortcut or via the application menus. You can also specify any number of arguments to log; just pass them as a comma-separated list:

```
console.log "Some math:", Math.PI, Math.E
console.error "Danger! Danger! "
```

A sample of the console output as viewed in the Chrome Developer Tools is shown in Figure 2.2.

Figure 2.2. The Chrome Developer Tools console

Debugging with CoffeeScript can sometimes be more difficult than you'd expect, as the errors that are displayed are based on the *final compiled code*, rather than your source code. This means that line numbers will fail to match up, and is one reason for having some familiarity with the JavaScript that's spat out.

There is new technology slowly filtering into browsers called "source maps" that will help map source code to the compiled output for debugging purposes; however, until there's widespread support, we'll have to make do with reading JavaScript and making good use of `console.log`!

---

[1] http://www.browserstack.com/debugging-tools

Returning to JavaScript

Learning a new language can sometimes be a frustrating experience. You know *exactly* how to perform a task in one language, but have no idea how to do it in the new one. CoffeeScript gives you a fallback if you really need it, a way to embed pieces of JavaScript directly in your CoffeeScript source. Any text wrapped in backticks or grave accents [`] will simply be passed straight through to the JavaScript output. For example, this is CoffeeScript:

```
greeter = `function(name) {
  console.log("Hello, " + name);
}`
```

The JavaScript output generated from it is as follows:

```
var greeter;

greeter = function(name) {
  console.log("Hello, " + name);
};
```

Notice that anything inside the backticks is handed on exactly as typed, but everything around it is compiled as usual. It's to be hoped that you wouldn't resort to this feature too often, but it's nice to know it's there.

Strings

A lot of today's web development involves string manipulation, and currently JavaScript has some clunky string handling. Much of the clunk is due to be repaired in the ECMAScript 6 specification, but until then, CoffeeScript is here to smooth over the rough patches.

The first feature CoffeeScript adds is multiline strings. To use this feature, simply utilize your enter key:

```
lastSentence = "To use this
    feature, simply utilize
    your enter key"
```

To use quotes in the string itself, you'll have to escape them with a backslash. When compiled, the multiline string will simply be concatenated into a one-liner. If that's not what you're after, and you want to keep your formatting (or you just want to avoid the hassle of escaping away your double quotes), you can use the block string feature employing triple double quotes:

```
haiku = """
  I mean, we're looking
  Down on Wayne's basement. Only
  That's not Wayne's basement
"""
```

The final and coolest string bonus on offer with CoffeeScript is **string interpolation**. Many of the examples we've seen have already demonstrated this concept; it's the ability to easily embed values in the middle of double-quoted strings (including the multiline and block strings), without laborious string concatenation:

```
name = "Steak Styles"
score = 8675308
display = "Player #{name} has #{score++} points"
```

A token is formed by wrapping an expression with #{ and }. These tokens are replaced in the compiled output in a manner that resembles how you'd probably do it in plain old JavaScript:

```
var display = "Player " + name + " has " + (score++) + " points";
```

That's a lot of pluses and quotes. It's a minor pain to both read and write, especially when building complicated expressions. CoffeeScript's string interpolation takes that pain away.

Conditionals and Operators

Our language wouldn't be "Turing complete"[2] without some conditional branching. Naturally, it's straightforward, but there are a few extras in CoffeeScript to make our code more concise, readable, and fun:

---

[2] http://en.wikipedia.org/wiki/Turing_completeness

```
if lives == 0
  alert "Game Over!"
  running = false
else
  frameCount += 1
```

Like function calls, the parentheses are missing, and we have to indent to start a new code block. However, if it's just a simple one-liner, you can join the statements with the then keyword, or put the expression first (this inverted or post-fix form comes up a lot in CoffeeScript). The following two lines compile to exactly the same JavaScript:

```
if lives == 0 then alert "Game Over"
```

```
alert "Game Over" if lives == 0
```

Oftentimes, you'll simply be using if statements to test a condition before assigning a value to a variable. CoffeeScript lacks the ternary construct (which in C-like languages allows you to do statements such as danger = (distance < 0) ? "HIGH" : "LOW"); rather, it uses the same if structure as above:

```
danger = if distance < 10 then "HIGH" else "LOW"
```

And if the else clause is unnecessary, there's even a nicer construct for conditional assignments:

```
danger = "HIGH" if distance < 10
```

Operator Aliases

You only need a small amount of JavaScript coding under your belt before its concepts of "truthiness" and "falsiness" bite you. The idea of true and false seems so binary, but there are some crazy aspects to it in JavaScript stemming from distinct types and values evaluating true or false differently; this in turn makes equality-testing bug-prone. For example, an empty string evaluates to false and an undefined value also evaluates to false, so you need to be careful how you test.

To guarantee equality on these types, you can use JavaScript's triple equals operator [===] rather than the regular double equals [==]. This is a good idea that helps avoid nasty logic bugs, so naturally CoffeeScript bakes this right in, compiling == into === and != into !==, and you don't have to worry about it.

But there's more: a whole slew of JavaScript operators are aliased for your comfort too, though instead of symbols, they're aliased to their English-language equivalents. For example, JavaScript's not (!), and (&&), and or (||) operators are aliased to not, and, and or! Consider the following:

```
drawGlow() if (running and energy > 10) or poweredUp
```

Not everyone is going to be thrilled with this literate style, though some will love it. The reasoning behind these operators is to help write code that you (and other people working with your code) can easily read. If you were born and raised with pipes and ampersands, you might think changing to prose is a useless feature, but give it a go.

If you find yourself liking it, here are a few more to add to the mix: is and isnt are aliases for == and != (which, as we said, is an alias for the triple equals versions); on and yes are the equivalent of true; and off and no are both the same as false. Finally, the inverse of if is aliased to unless, letting us write code such as:

```
power = on unless lives is 0
```

This will compile down to:

```
var power;
if (lives !== 0) {
  power = true;
}
```

Again, all these are optional; it's up to your personal style. You might like to use the aliases when testing against variable names, and regular symbols when testing numbers, for example.

Loops and Ranges

We've already used a few `for` loops in the examples and by the time we've finished the game, we'll be almost sick of them. Tile-based games are rooted in a 2D grid, therefore you spend a lot of time inside nested loops: the outside loop to iterate over the `rows` of the grid, and the inside loop for the `columns`. However, for most other work such as web development, we won't use loops as much as we do in game development; this is because we process our lists using comprehensions, a concise notation for specifying operations over a list, which we'll look at fully in the section called "List Comprehensions" in Chapter 3.

The loops we've used so far have been defined using ranges, where our loop iterates over the values inside the range. Just like the `if` statement, we can either write an indented code block, or use the inverse form for simple expressions:

```
console.log "GO!" for [1..3]
```

This will give us three `"GO!"`s on the console. You have the option to break out of a `for` loop or continue on to the next iteration with `break` and `continue`—exactly the same as in JavaScript. In many cases, we'll want to have access to the current index the loop is in. To do this, we assign the current value to a variable:

```
console.log "...and a #{ x }" for x in [1..4]
```

These kinds of range loops will be compiled into regular `for` loops, albeit with a hidden temporary variable: this is to allow anything we throw at CoffeeScript to be handled generically:

```
var x, _i;

for (x = _i = 1; _i <= 4; x = ++_i) {
  console.log("...and a " + x);
}
```

Inclusive versus Exclusive Ranges

Notice that the range loop includes the start and end figure. If your programmer brain dislikes the last number being included, you can use the triple-period syntax:

[0...4]; this gives us the numbers 0 to 3, more like the for loops you might be used to!

Ranges do not have to be ascending. If you want a descending range, simply put the larger number as the first argument, and the smaller as the second. And if you need a different size step between loops, you can specify it with the by keyword after the range, remembering to use the correct sign:

```
for x in [99..1] by -2
  console.log "#{x} bottles of beer on the wall"
```

If our logic to execute is a short one-liner, we can use the post-fix form in the same way we did for our conditionals:

```
console.log x for x in [1..10]
```

But for is not the only way to move in a circle: CoffeeScript also provides a low-level while loop. Like our operator alias, we also have a "while not" version: until. These can be used as traditional while loops, or in post-fix form for prose-like readability:

```
animatePlayer() while alive
fall() until yPosition is 0
```

The final looping loop is loop; use it if you want to loop forever. Well, nothing lasts *forever*: it's just a while(true){} that can be broken with break:

```
loop
  killBaddie()
  break if baddieCount is 0
```

Comprehensive Collectivism

The constructs we've covered here should be familiar to programmers of imperative languages like Java or C; however, CoffeeScript favors using comprehensions over low-level loops. The idea is to abstract away the technical process of looping and concentrate on processing a collection as if it were a single item. This leads to shorter, more expressive code—so stay tuned!

Objects and Arrays

Okay, we can control our program flow, but what about data structures? We have `Arrays` for lists, and `Objects` for key/value dictionaries; what more do we need? Arrays are defined by wrapping your comma-separated list in square brackets:

```
blocks = ["dirt", "stone", "coal", "iron ore"]
console.log blocks.length # 4
```

Each array element can be of any type (including other arrays), and whitespace is ignored; the compiled version will be concatenated into one long line. If you include line breaks, the trailing comma on each line is optional. This is useful when you're defining lists that will be processed one-dimensionally, but are better represented visually in two dimensions (quite common for games):

```
levelMap1 = [
  1,1,1,1,1
  1,0,0,0,1
  1,0,1,0,1
  1,0,0,0,1
  1,1,1,1,1
]
```

Naturally, all the `Array`'s built-in properties and methods are available: `push`, `pop`, `reverse`, `join`, `concat` ... it's all there. Additionally, CoffeeScript provides some helpers for slicing, dicing, and processing arrays, the most notable being able to use them directly in `for` loops:

```
register block for block in ["dirt", "stone", "coal"]
```

The `for ... in` construct will call the `register` function on each string in our array, as did the range loops above. One difference is that for our regular arrays, we might also want to know the current index the loop is in. We do this by supplying an extra variable, separated by a comma:

```
topPlayers = ["Max", "Lily", "Brian", "Tracy"]
for player, i in topPlayers
  console.log "Rank: #{ i }. Player: #{ player }"
```

Now, on to objects! At their base, objects are a collection of key/value pairs. They're a fundamental method of encapsulation in CoffeeScript, allowing us to group related functionality together in a single location. Objects are structured by indentation, though braces are optional—but particularly useful when you only need a small object that can be defined on a single line:

```
player =
  x: 10
  y: 25
  stats:
    score: 1337
  update: (speed) ->
    @x += speed
    @stats.score += 5
```

The `player` object contains a bunch of key/value pairs: `x`, and `y` as numbers, `stats` as a nested object, and `update` as a function. The outside world can interact with the object directly via its name:

```
player.update 2.5
```

Inside the `update` function, you'll notice the variable names commence with an `@`, which is an alias for `this.`, a keyword used to indicate the current scope. Scope is a hairy issue in JavaScript, so we'll talk about this some more later; for now, you can see that prefixing an identifier with the `@` symbol means we're referring to the identifier in the current scope. In our example, the `update` function will compile as:

```
this.x += speed;
this.stats.score += 5;
```

This will update the player properties accordingly.

Reserved Words as Keys

In JavaScript, there's a small army of reserved words that each perform a certain task. Normally, these words must be quoted if you're going to use them as keys in your object; but, once again, CoffeeScript has us covered. If you happen to use a reserved word, it'll be automagically quoted.

We can iterate over an object in a similar way that we did for `Arrays`, but this time using the `for … of` construct:

```
for own key, value of player
  console.log "#{key}: #{value}"
```

You can choose any identifier for the `key` and `value` variables. Notice the `own` keyword in there? This is optional, and used to counter another fun gotcha from JavaScript: looping over the keys of an object that were defined directly, rather than being inherited (for each key, it tests the object's `hasOwnProperty(key)` function under the covers).

Introducing Professor Digman-Rünner

It's well into the afternoon, with minimal movement from the team. One email from the pixel artist says she refuses to draw anything until there's a theme, and there's a strange tweet from the story writer saying he had the most amazing idea for the game last night, but he struggles to recall it now. Fed up, you crack open your image editor, set the pencil tool to one pixel, and draw like you've never drawn before (which is true), as evident in Figure 2.3.

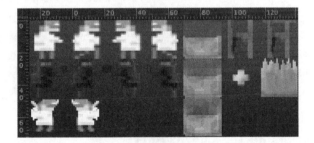

Figure 2.3. Creating our game characters

Okay, that's extremely retro, but it's something. Looks like we have a guy in a lab coat wearing safety goggles, and a ninja …

And like a flash, it all becomes clear: Welcome to the world of "Professor Digman-Rünner: Particle Physicist"![3] The Professor is hot on the trail of the infamous elementary particle, the Pig's Boffin. After years of study at the "Digman-Rünner Re-

---

[3] I wanted this blinking, but SitePoint told me it was impractical.

search Institute for Research," he's finally proven the existence of the elusive particle and is ready to announce it to the scientific community.

Alas, there is trouble afoot. His archenemy and nemesis, Stealthy HawkMan, has a lucrative book-publishing deal in the works for his personal memoirs, the majority of which is just him making fun of the Professor's study of Pig's Boffin. If the Professor were to release his findings to the public, his archenemy's book deal would fall through, forcing Stealthy HawkMan to continue in the teaching position he despises. Using his international HawkMan family connections, Stealthy organizes a team of Japanese ninjas (frozen in time since the Meiji Restoration of 1868) to steal the Professor's particle research.

Luckily, the ninjas are relatively unfamiliar with the Standard Model of particle physics. This provides the Professor with an opportunity to reclaim his work using his two superpowers (which he's been secretly developing over the years). His primary superpower of running will be handy to escape the ninjas, while his secondary power will enable him to dig traps in the laboratory floor that will ensnare unsuspecting ninjas. It's all up to Professor Digman-Rünner. Good luck.

The Canvas API

Clearly, we're going to require some graphics for our game. And for that, we'll have to step out of the laboratory in order to become familiar with the HTML5 Canvas API. We don't need to *master* it (indeed, for our immediate purposes we just want to place our professor and some ninjas on the screen), but it's a fairly simple API, and we'll use more of it when it comes time to add flourishes.

 CoffeeScript and the Canvas API

How are CoffeeScript and the Canvas API related? If you're just starting out with web development, it's easy to be confused about the separate parts. The Canvas DOM element was introduced as part of HTML5. To draw on the canvas, you use various drawing and manipulation methods via its API, which you access in the browser via JavaScript. And as we know, if we can target it with JavaScript, we can also target it with CoffeeScript!

The Canvas API requires some boilerplate setup, and a place to live. Let's add a new Coffee file, called **gfx.coffee**, to hold our graphics container object; this will include a bunch of helpful properties and methods that we'll access often. For now, we'll just set up a blank `init` function as an entrance point:

chapter02/src/gfx.coffee (excerpt)

```
gfx =
  init: ->
```

We'll add this to our list of files that `coffee` is watching too:

```
coffee -j ../script/main.js -w -c gfx.coffee game.coffee
```

Check the compiled **main.js** file and make sure you can see a reference to our `gfx` object.

Context and Soaking up Nulls

To draw shapes and graphics on the screen, any and all drawing operations must be done on a canvas's `context`. Usually, you'll grab this context when your application initializes and either keep a reference to it, or pass it around your functions that need it. To obtain the reference, ask for it from the canvas DOM element in your web page using `getContext`:

chapter02/src/gfx.coffee (excerpt)

```
init: ->
  canvasDOM = document.getElementById "game"
  @ctx = canvasDOM.getContext "2d"
```

This will give you a 2D context to draw in (store it in the `gfx` object as `ctx`), assuming there's a document element, the document contains a `<canvas id="game"></canvas>` tag, *and* the user's browser actually supports the Canvas API.

But what if any of these assumptions are incorrect? If either of the first two assumptions is incorrect, the next line will fail; if the last is incorrect, any use of `ctx` will fail. In all cases, the user will be left wondering what the heck is going on.

We'll have to let the user know if there's a problem, and abort the running of the game. We could do that by returning `true` or `false` from our `init` function to indicate if initialization was successful:

```
                                        chapter02/src/gfx.coffee (excerpt)
init: ->
  canvasDOM = document.getElementById "game"
  @ctx = canvasDOM.getContext "2d" if canvasDOM != null
  return @ctx == null
```

This works, and stops our code from crashing if something is amiss. However, CoffeeScript provides us with a way to do it that's more concise, and without requiring the declaration of intermediate temporary variables:

```
                                        chapter02/src/gfx.coffee (excerpt)
init: ->
  canvas = document.querySelector "#game"
  @ctx = canvas?.getContext? "2d"
  @ctx?
```

We use the ? operator on a variable to "soak up nulls." If the value is null, the code keeps running, and we can handle any errors afterwards. The ? operator can also be used to assign default values. For example, to select and assign the DOM element only if the canvas element was yet to be assigned already, we could do this:

```
canvas = canvas ? document.querySelector "#game"
```

Though, in this situation, it seems redundant to have to assign canvas to itself like this, so we can use the shortcut version instead:

```
canvas ?= document.querySelector "#game"
```

What if document is missing?

In reality, if there is no document or the document.getElementById fails, you have bigger problems—something has gone seriously wrong. For a regular project, this is unnecessary; just checking the context, which some browsers won't support, should be sufficient.

Back in our main **game.coffee** file, we can now initialize our canvas element and notify the user if the initialization failed:

```
                          chapter02/src/game.coffee (excerpt)

game =
  init: ->
    if not gfx.init()
      alert "Could not set up game canvas!"
      return # abort the game

# Start the game running
game.init()
```

With the initialization out of the way, we can start to find out more about our game canvas. The `context` contains a field called `canvas`, which in turn contains its own `width` and `height` fields. However, since we already have a reference to `canvas`, we can access the `width` and `height` fields directly. We'll be using these often, so let's expand our `gfx` object and attach some shortcuts:

```
                          chapter02/src/gfx.coffee (excerpt)

init: ->
  canvas = document.querySelector "#game"
  @ctx = canvas?.getContext? "2d"
  return false if not @ctx
  @w = canvas.width
  @h = canvas.height
  true
```

Now that we're reasonably sure we have a place to draw, let's start with a clean slate by clearing our canvas using the `clearRect` method:

```
                          chapter02/src/gfx.coffee (excerpt)

gfx.ctx.clearRect 0, 0, gfx.w, gfx.h
```

Actually, while we're at it, let's make that a helper method that we can add directly to our `gfx` object:

```
                          chapter02/src/gfx.coffee (excerpt)

clear: -> @ctx.clearRect 0, 0, @w, @h
```

And then call it from the game code:

```
init: ->
  if not gfx.init()
    alert "Could not set up game canvas!"
    return # abort the game

  # Ready to play!
  gfx.clear()
```

The `clearRect` method removes any content from the rectangle specified by the arguments *x1*, *y1*, *x2*, and *y2*. In our example, we've emptied everything by clearing from the point `0, 0` (top left) to the point at `width` and `height` of the canvas (bottom right). In a game, this method is often called before each frame to erase the last frame's content. This is a bit unnecessary if you're going to fill the *entire* screen anyway; for example, if you're drawing a tiled map. However, be aware that transparent images can still cause issues. When in doubt, it's best to clear each frame and then optimize as your performance needs dictate.

Drawing Primitives

To draw shapes on the screen, we need to define the style properties of our `context` and then call the method that draws it. Generally, shapes can be either stroked (drawn as an outline) or filled (colored in), and the styles must be defined separately for either. While we won't be using this code in the upcoming sections, feel free to experiment by appending it to the end of your **game.coffee** file. (Make sure to delete it or comment it out when you're done experimenting.) Here's an example of filling and then stroking a rectangle:

```
c = gfx.ctx
c.fillStyle = "orange"
c.fillRect 10, 10, 300, 80
c.strokeStyle = "#3f3f3f"
c.strokeRect 10, 10, 300, 80
```

Context Is Important

You *always* need a context to draw in, and for our game that context is always going to be `gfx.ctx`. Because we sometimes need to perform a lot of operations on the context, we'll often alias `gfx.ctx` to `c`, just to keep the code shorter.

And that's all there is to it if your end goal is to make an orange rectangle with a dark-gray border!

The `fillRect` and `strokeRect` methods both accept four parameters: the *x* and *y* coordinates of the top-left corner of the rectangle, and the width and height of the rectangle. Although our rectangle looks like a single item, it actually requires two separate drawing operations; we just happen to use the same parameter values for each.

For our game, we'll certainly have to draw some text. Just like the rectangle, we specify some styles, then fill or stroke the text:

chapter02/src/game.coffee (excerpt)

```
c.fillStyle = "#202020"
c.font = "14pt monospace"
c.fillText "Professor Digman-Rünner", 30, 55
```

Aaaand … Figure 2.4 reveals our title screen! The `fillText` method takes a string to draw, and an (x, y) coordinate from which to start drawing.

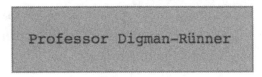

Figure 2.4. Basic title screen

The Canvas API offers plenty more than this: creating (and stroking or filling) paths, arcs (for circles), Bézier curves, a host of gradient fill options, text metrics (for measuring strings for alignment) … and lots more. We'll address them as we need them, but if you find yourself wondering if such-and-such a feature exists, the API is very consistent and these basics scale well. Head over to the spec and find out more![4]

Draw an Image

We have no intention of creating our graphics out of squares and circles—that's too much work. We want our pixel artist to hand us a bunch of amazing graphics and we'll render them instead. Though, with our pixel artist still missing in action, we have our blocky professor and ninjas to tide us over.

Our game is going to be tile-based: which means the background will be a grid composed of a handful of tiles rather than one great big image. We'll create all our levels out of these tiles. We've chosen (rather randomly) 24×24 pixel tiles. Historically, the size of tiles has been constrained to powers of two to fit in the smallest number of machine bytes; however, we have no limitations on the desktop, so you can choose whatever you like. 24×24 and 32×32 are still very common for pixel-art games, though.

We've created some tiles—the ground block and a ladder—as well as some character images. On-screen character images in 2D video games are called **sprites**. When we push all our art together in a fixed-size grid, as we have done, we call it a **sprite sheet**. In our game, we draw the correct subsection of the sprite sheet to the screen for each tile and character. It's a very handy way to keep all our assets together, as well as reduce our game's loading time.

To put our image on canvas, we need an image source to draw. You might be hoping to simply reference our PNG file by providing the URL as a string, but, unfortunately, canvas doesn't work that way. The source must be either a DOM image or another canvas object. This means we have to take care of loading the image manually and making sure it has loaded before we try to draw it.

The most common approach to resource loading is to dynamically create an image, and hook into its `load` event. If you have a bunch of images to load, you'll have to be a bit cleverer, or consider using a dedicated resource loader. In this case, we'll just save our image to our `gfx` object and provide a callback that runs when our image is loaded:

---

[4] http://www.whatwg.org/specs/web-apps/current-work/multipage/the-canvas-element.html

chapter02/src/gfx.coffee *(excerpt)*

```coffee
load: (onload) ->
  @sprites = new Image()
  @sprites.src = "resources/sprites.png"
  @sprites.onload = -> onload()
```

When we call `load`, we provide a function once our image is ready. This will be where we start running the game and perform other initialization work; for now, let's just start drawing directly inside the callback. Underneath our context check, add the following call:

chapter02/src/game.coffee *(excerpt)*

```coffee
init: ->
  ⋮
  gfx.load ->
    c = gfx.ctx
    c.drawImage gfx.sprites, 10, 20
```

The `drawImage` function takes the image we want to draw, and an *x* and *y* screen position. Our example draws the sprites ten pixels in from the left, and 20 pixels down from the top.

Processing a Sprite Sheet

Drawing the entire image will be useful for drawing title screens, menu backgrounds, and the like, but no good for drawing our sprites. We need to be able to extract and draw just a slice of each image for each tile and character. The `drawImage` method has another signature for this very purpose:

```coffee
drawImage image, sx, sy, sw, sh, dx, dy, dw, dh
```

This version takes an image, then two sets of coordinates: a source rectangle and a destination rectangle. The source rectangle specifies where we want our slice to start (`sx`, `sy`), and how much of the image we want to copy (`sw`, `sh`). Having defined the area to copy, we then define where to paste it (`dx`, `dy`), and how big the final image should be (`dw`, `dh`). If we make the destination width and height different from the source width and height, it will be stretched to fit (which can be cool for crazy effects!).

Calculating the slice coordinates for each sprite is a pain, and will be required frequently, so let's make it into another method of our `gfx` object. The drawing context and the sprite image are stored here, so we can refer to them using the alias, `@`:

chapter02/src/gfx.coffee *(excerpt)*

```
drawSprite: (col, row, x, y) ->
  @ctx.drawImage @sprites,
    col * 24, row * 24, 24, 24,
    x, y, 24, 24
```

With a tiny amount of math, we can calculate our slice from a given row and column of the sprite sheet. The tiles are 24×24 pixels, hence the abundance of 24s: each slice is column × tile-width wide, and row × tile-height tall. To test it out, let's give our Professor his first solo performance on the screen:

chapter02/src/game.coffee *(excerpt)*

```
gfx.load: ->
  ⋮
  gfx.drawSprite 0, 0, 100, 50
```

Figure 2.5 shows the result.

Figure 2.5. Professor performs a solo

The Professor lives at the top of our sprite sheet, and his first frame is in column 0 and row 0. Whenever we want to draw a sprite, we have to count its row and column, and give it the *x* and *y* position to start drawing from. Simple as that!

Random Map

The day is starting to drag on, and having done the hard work of placing a character onscreen, it's time to have a little fun. By now, this should be relatively easy to follow:

chapter02/src/game.coffee *(excerpt)*

```
gfx.load: ->
  ⋮
  rand = (max) -> Math.floor Math.random() * max
  for y in [0..19]
    for x in [0..23]
      col = rand 7
      row = rand 2
      gfx.drawSprite col, row, x * 24, y * 24
```

And that pixelated Andy Warhol effort seen in Figure 2.6 is the basis of our game!

Figure 2.6. Our grid takes shape, to Warholian effect

Rather than randomly draw tiles, we'll design the grid with love and care. There are a bunch of magic numbers in that snippet (which we'll deal with soon): we are drawing 20 rows and 24 columns (counting from 0), and choosing a tile from the sprite sheet by selecting a random row and column (we only have two rows at the moment). The little rand function is a helper to return a random integer between 0 and max, so we can avoid repeating those unsightly math functions.

 Feeling adventurous?

Here are a few tests for consolidating what we've covered:

- Make a random map featuring only the dirt and stone tiles.

- Create the '70s disco from Chapter 1, but with sprites instead of rectangles (hint: remember to clear the context!).

- Write a random number helper that accepts both a min and a max. Extra points if min is optional. Use it to draw a map sans the Professor or ninjas.

Ready to Rumble

We now have full control over our code and pixels, and are ready to rumble. Having covered and mastered the essential basics of CoffeeScript, we can start using CoffeeScript for all our coding needs. Well, mostly … there's still a lot of powerful functionality to uncover. And with our 7-day HTML5 Game Jam-a-Thon Challenge (TM) team proving unreliable, we're going to need all the help we can get!

Chapter 3

Features to Boost Your Game

It's certainly been a whirlwind couple of days and we now have the basics of Coffee-Script under our belts. While the basics are fun, it's the more advanced aspects of the language that make it interesting. In this chapter, we'll apply the basics for our game to work, and make a start exploring the more interesting parts as we go: advanced module and function features, and the all-powerful list comprehensions.

Team Meeting

You pitch your game idea and initial mockups, and naturally the team is in love with the "Professor Digman-Rünner" concept; they've already started planning spin-offs and talking about merchandising and franchising options.

The story writer is very intrigued with the history of the Professor, and the tapestry of rich characters that will support him. The pixel artist is excited about the rough work you've started and is chattering about color theory and radical shading possibilities. Everyone (except yourself) agrees that they need to think about it for a while, and promptly depart the café, leaving you to stare at your to-do list filled with unassigned tasks.

Having already established the groundwork of a tile-based map yesterday, you decide that the focus for today will be creating levels and maps. Once we have our levels working, we'll want to populate them with the Professor, too, and control him with the keyboard. And if we have any time left over, we should also start looking for some new team members. Busy day ahead!

Functions Revisited

Functions, being first-class citizens, are already powerful in JavaScript, and CoffeeScript adds some syntactic niceness that makes working with functions even more enjoyable. Let's take another look at the ways we can define various functions:

```
square = (x) -> x * x
distance = (x1, y1, x2, y2) ->
  diff = square(x1 - x2) + square(y1 - y2)
  Math.sqrt diff
test = -> alert distance(2, 3, 5, 5)
```

The first function, `square`, simply squares a number and returns the value. The function body is included inline with the function definition. Notice how much more the actual logic of the function jumps out at the reader, compared to the JavaScript equivalent in the snippet that follows, which is shrouded in long keywords and assorted other symbols (this is particularly a problem when doing functional-style programming, where programs are composed of many small functions):

```
function square(x) {
  return x * x;
}
```

The next function we define, `distance`, takes four parameters: the x and y coordinates of, say, a bad guy in our game, and the x and y coordinates of our trusty hero. It then calculates the distance between the two entities using Pythagoras' Theorem (and using our `square` function). This very useful piece of math tells us how far away the bad guys are! We define the function body as a block by indenting it.

The final example, `test`, is a function that takes no parameters and simply alerts a test run of our `distance` function. Because everything is an expression, the result of the alert is actually returned from the function (though the result of `alert` is always `undefined`). Notice, too, that the parentheses are optional:

```
test = () -> alert "this is ok, too!"
```

Default Argument Values

Our drawSprite method is quite cool, as it lets us draw any of our tiles on the screen, wherever we want. However, we'd like to make it more powerful, and be able to specify the width and height of the source tile space (for example, so we could draw a big tile in one operation), as well as specifying the scale to draw the tiles. Let's begin a new function that handles these tasks:

chapter03/src/gfx.coffee (excerpt)

```
drawSpriteFancy: (col, row, x, y, w, h, scale) -> # do the work
```

If we call drawSpriteFancy like this:

```
gfx.drawSpriteFancy(0, 0, 10, 10, 2, 2, 2)
```

… we want it to draw a 2×2 tile area to the screen (at position 10, 10) and scale it to twice the height. To achieve this behavior, we'll first add the tile width and height constants in our gfx object. Because we'll be working a lot with grids, we'll be using this to calculate offsets, rather than have magic numbers everywhere that could change if, say, the pixel artist wants to use 32×24 pixel tiles for the final graphics:

chapter03/src/gfx.coffee (excerpt)

```
gfx =
  tileW: 24
  tileH: 24
```

Now we'll use these values to calculate the coordinates of the pixels we draw by multiplying the number of tiles by the tile width and height (and in the process do away with all our magic numbers):

chapter03/src/gfx.coffee (excerpt)

```
drawSpriteFancy: (col, row, x, y, w, h, scale) ->
  w *= @tileW
  h *= @tileH
```

```
@ctx.drawImage @sprites,
  col * w, row * h, w, h,
  x, y, w * scale, h * scale
```

Awesome! But it seems a bit of a shame that we need two functions that do basically the same job. Our original `drawSprite` method is just a call to `drawSpriteFancy` with w, h, and `scale` being 1. It's time to introduce **default arguments**! Default arguments let us specify a value to use if the calling code fails to pass a value of its own. To combine our two sprite drawing functions, we remove the old `drawSprite` function, and modify the `drawSpriteFancy` function like so:

chapter03/src/gfx.coffee *(excerpt)*

```
drawSprite: (col, row, x, y, w = 1, h = 1, scale = 1) ->
  w *= @tileW
  h *= @tileH
  @ctx.drawImage @sprites,
    col * w, row * h, w, h,
    x, y, w * scale, h * scale
```

We can assign a value directly to the parameter name. When calling the function, if we fail to supply w, h, and `scale` arguments, they'll be magically set for us. In our game, this is perfect. For the majority of the time, we'll want normal-size tiles. Feel free to replace the contents of the `gfx.load` callback (but keep the `rand` function!), as we won't be needing a screen full of random tiles any longer. From the callback, we can call `drawSprite` as usual:

chapter03/src/game.coffee *(excerpt)*

```
gfx.drawSprite(0, 0, 50, 50)
```

Then, when we want the extra features, we just add in the extra parameters, overriding the height, width, scale, or all of the optional arguments. Here's a version that will draw a two-tile-high image with the default scale:

chapter03/src/game.coffee *(excerpt)*

```
gfx.drawSprite(0, 0, 74, 50, 1, 1, 2)
```

Then, Figure 3.1 shows the result.

Figure 3.1. The two-tile-high club

 Win By Default

When compiled, the JavaScript simply checks if the argument is `null`. If so, it assigns the default value—so it's more useful and natural to only include defaults for the trailing arguments (or all arguments), otherwise the client code would have to explicitly pass `null`s to get the defaults. For example, if we removed the default value from the final scale argument, we'd have to call `drawSprite(0, 0, 10, 10, null, null, 2)` for the default `width` and `height`.

Function Gotchas

There are a couple of gotchas when writing functions that you should be aware of, especially when starting out. The first is because of the optional parentheses:

```
strategy () -> # do something
strategy() -> # do something
```

Despite having only a one-space difference, these two declarations perform very different operations. The first calls the `strategy` function with one parameter, that being the anonymous function. The second calls `strategy` with zero parameters, and applies the anonymous function to the result of `strategy` (the result would itself have to be a function for this code to work). The difference is much more obvious if we also include the optional empty parentheses for the second call:

```
strategy() () -> #do something
```

The second gotcha involves lining up your code blocks when using anonymous functions as parameters. For example, the `setTimeout` function accepts two parameters: a function to call, and a time delay to wait until it calls the function:

```
setTimeout functionName, delayInMilliseconds
```

If you want the function to be an inline anonymous function, you have to be careful with the parameters that follow:

```
setTimeout ->
  if goalsAttained is 0
    alert "Time expired!"
  else
    nextGoal()
, 2000
```

Like always, to finish a code block you have to "unindent"; however, unlike always, the next symbol is a comma. This can look a bit weird, so some people like to wrap the entire block in parentheses to make it more obvious. This can also be used to do inline functions:

```
setTimeout (-> alert "Time expired!"), 2000
```

A related gotcha is common when **chaining function calls**. Function chaining is very useful when processing lists and the result of each operation is a new list on which further operations can be performed. This will be particularly familiar to developers who've used jQuery (which we'll cover in the section called "Using jQuery" in Chapter 6) where function chaining is an addictive habit! You might be tempted to write your chains like this:

```
badGuys
  .attack player1
  .moveTo 10, 10
```

But there's a problem here, and the actual compiled output would be:

```
badGuys.attack(player1.moveTo(10, 10));
```

Notice that the chain is broken and the moveTo function is applied to the player1 object? If you think of your chains as a single line of code, the problem is more obvious. And the solution again is that you need to include the parentheses:

```
badGuys
  .attack(player1)
  .moveTo(10, 10)
```

List Comprehensions

The `for` loops that we looked at in the section called "Loops and Ranges" in Chapter 2 have some superpowers that make working with lists of data a joy (if you're into that kind of thing). They are **list comprehensions** that create new lists from themselves—allowing you to easily manipulate and process your data with minimal amounts of boilerplate-looping syntax.

The trick to list comprehensions in CoffeeScript is that loops, like nearly every expression, will also return a result. This might seem a bit weird; that is, what's the result of a loop? Under the hood, CoffeeScript will create a new array and push the result of each loop iteration into it, and thus form a list of the processed data. Very nifty! To use it, simply wrap the `for` loop in parentheses (hmm, this is starting to sound familiar!); then return the value you want from the parenthesized expression.

We need a fitting example to show the stealthy power of our `for` expression—and what's more stealthy than a bunch of ninjas? Let's plot a bunch of them randomly on the screen, with the assistance of a couple of helper functions:

chapter03/src/game.coffee *(excerpt)*

```
makeANinja = () ->
  x: rand gfx.w
  y: rand gfx.h

drawANinja = (n) -> gfx.drawSprite 0, 1, n.x, n.y

ninjas = (makeANinja() for [0...20])
```

We have one function—`makeANinja`—that returns an object containing a random number (using our `rand` function from the section called "Random Map" in Chapter 2) between 0 and the canvas `width`, and another random number between 0 and the canvas `height`. The next function draws a ninja (the tile at position 0 of row 1) at a random position on the screen.

Our comprehension calls our ninja factory in each iteration of the loop, and pushes it to the resulting array. And hey presto: 20 ninjas held in our custom storage facility (well, a regular old array). The comprehension expression does not have to be a function; whatever value you put here will be added to the array, though it does work particularly nicely as a factory, and we'll be using this more as we progress through the game.

But the ninjas might be a bit *too* stealthy for us at the moment, because they're completely invisible. Let's coax them out of their hiding places and draw them on the screen from our `gfx.load` callback:

chapter03/src/game.coffee *(excerpt)*

```
drawANinja n for n in ninjas
```

Ah! We can now see them in Figure 3.2.

Figure 3.2. Ninjas coming out to play

We can feel more confident of our safety when they're in plain sight like that.

Comprehensions also allow us to use guard conditions to filter the results, using the when keyword. If we only wanted to see the ninjas on the left side of the screen, we could filter the list based on the ninja's x position:

chapter03/src/game.coffee *(excerpt)*

```
leftNinjas = (n for n in ninjas when n.x < gfx.w / 2)
drawANinja n for n in leftNinjas
```

Our guard condition tests that the ninja's x position is less than half the canvas width. When ninjas pass the test, they're added to the final list. We can draw the lucky winners as we did before.

We're applying the comprehensions to our ninja objects, but they work consistently for any data type; for example, if you wanted to find overly long name fields in your database, you could just filter them (the result will be an array containing the validation error message for each long name):

```
people = ["Smith", "Jones", "Castledine-Carlin"]
longNames = for name in people when name.length > 10
  "Validation error for person: #{name}"
```

JavaScript Alternatives

Comprehensions can be used to do `forEach`, `map`, and `filter`. These functions do exist in recent versions of JavaScript, and you can use them too, if you like—but they aren't quite as idiomatic as the constructs we just discussed.

Creating a Level

Time to get back to Professor Digman-Rünner. In the section called "Random Map" in Chapter 2, we had random tiles all over the screen, and our goal was to harness some order from the chaos and create a level. Most games will feature some kind of level editor to quickly build fun and exciting gameplay. We'll build our editor later when we need it; for now, we'd like to be able to draw some levels in ASCII, and have them rendered as tiles.

We'll start with the most entertaining part: sketching out a level. Add a new variable, `level1`, and make it a multiline string:

chapter03/src/game.coffee *(excerpt)*

```
level1 = """
  ..............
  ...........*.
  ....@#@@@@#@.
  .....#....#..
  .....#....#..
  ..*..#...@@@.
  ..@@@@@...#..
  ...#......#..
  ...#......#..
  ...#......#..
  .000000000000
"""
```

If you squint your eyes, you might just be able to figure out what that is—a small level! Each character represents a different tile in the game: the @ symbol is dirt, the # symbol is a ladder, the * is a magic particle ... and so on. It's a fairly low-tech way to go about level design, but it's a start!

Next, we have to map our level to the corresponding tiles in our sprite sheet. For now, we'll make a function that accepts our ASCII map and returns a 2D array of tile coordinates. Create the makeLevel function that will do three tasks:

chapter03/src/game.coffee (excerpt)

```
makeLevel = (ascii) ->
  # 1. Define the tile-to-symbol map
  # 2. Cut up the ASCII string into characters
  # 3. Map the characters to their tiles
```

The first step is to define an object that will map the characters to sprite sheet co-ordinates:

chapter03/src/game.coffee (excerpt)

```
# 1. Define the tile-to-symbol map
tiles =
  "@": [4, 1]
  "0": [4, 0]
  "*": [5, 1]
  "#": [5, 0]
```

If we ask for tiles["@"], it gives us the array [4, 1], which matches the fifth sprite on the second row: the dirt image.

The next step is to chop up the ASCII string. If you look in the compiled source for level1 (or read the section on strings), you'll see that the string is just one great big long line, and any line breaks are escaped as "\n" new-line characters. If we split the string at each row (using JavaScript's split function), we'll have an array of strings. If we then split each of these rows into characters, there will be a 2D array of the tile symbols. Here's a cunning comprehension to do just that:

chapter03/src/game.coffee *(excerpt)*

```
# 2. Cut up the ASCII string
asciiMap = (row.split "" for row in ascii.split "\n")
```

 By the By

In the section called "Loops and Ranges" in Chapter 2 covering "plain old" `for` loops, we saw that you can use the keyword **by** to step over each range in different-sized jumps—and of course, it works here too. Doing `ascii.split "\n" by 2` would make our levels half the height by skipping every second line!

This is a great example of the expressive power of comprehensions: it's doing a lot of work in few characters, but its function is still very clear. With our 2D array in hand, we can move on to the final step of mapping each cell to the tile coordinates. Another comprehension will help us here, and the list it produces becomes the output of the function:

chapter03/src/game.coffee *(excerpt)*

```
# 3. Map the characters to their tiles
(for row in asciiMap
  for col in row
    tiles[col])
```

For each row of the `asciiMap`, each cell is mapped to the tile coordinates and returned. If no tile is found—which will be the case for some of our periods—it returns a `null`, giving us our final (very simple) level model. Now we can move on to rendering it. For now, we'll do this straight inside the `gfx.load` callback function like we did in the section called "Draw an Image" in Chapter 2:

chapter03/src/game.coffee *(excerpt)*

```
# Create a map from the ascii
level = makeLevel level1

# Draw the level
for row, y in level
  for tile, x in row
    continue if not tile
```

```
    xPos = x * gfx.tileW
    yPos = y * gfx.tileH
    gfx.drawSprite tile[0], tile[1], xPos, yPos
```

This drawing code should look fairly familiar. It's exactly the same as our random map, but this time we're skipping over any nulls (so it leaves a blank space) and calculating the correct position using the tile width and height. The result is in Figure 3.3.

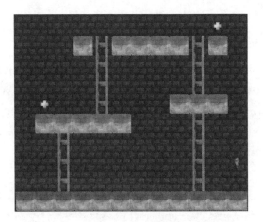

Figure 3.3. Stepping up to the platform

That has to make you giggle just a little bit: our ASCII doodling transformed into an awesome-looking platformer level! In the section called "Loading Levels" in Chapter 4, we'll refactor how we generate levels for our next set of goals—but all of the for comprehensions will stay with us.

Many day-to-day computing tasks involve filtering and transforming lists. The more you master comprehensions, the more you see how having a conventional interface for list processing is a very powerful feature. And once again, we'll be seeing a lot more of these guys before the game is done.

Building Larger Projects

The next step in our game is to handle player input and create a player module to hold our Professor. This necessitates adding two new files to keep things manageable and reusable for any games we make in the future (*cough* Professor Digman-Rünner: Re-dug *cough*). The filenames will have to be included in the compile step:

```
coffee -j ../script/main.js -w -c gfx.coffee keys.coffee player.cof
➥fee game.coffee
```

But adding the filename to `coffee` for *every* file will scale poorly—we could end up with hundreds of files to include! A simple option is to remove all the filenames and replace them with a wildcard:

```
coffee -j ../script/main.js -w -c .
```

This finds every file in the current directory and any subdirectories, and compiles them to the output file. This is a much nicer solution, because any new files we add to the project are automatically included and compiled as our project grows.

There's a problem, though: the `coffee` command reads directories from the file system alphabetically, so all the contained code will be imported and executed in this order. Most of the time, this is fine, because we namespace and modularize our code (like we did with the `gfx` object), and ensure everything has loaded before running any code. The fact that `gfx` is defined before `keys` won't matter.

However, if we have code that directly depends on other code (and we will if we have a base class or base object prototype), the order becomes important. We can't inherit traits from an object that's undefined, and so the code will break. A naive approach would be to simply name the files alphabetically (perhaps by adding an underscore to base objects), but that's a fairly dirty hack; we need a better solution.

Removing the Safety Wrapper

By default, CoffeeScript will wrap all your code in a "safety wrapper" to stop you leaking variables into the global namespace. In our project, we're careful to only expose our high-level objects; our game is running standalone, so we won't be interacting with other random code anyway. If we wanted to take matters into our own hands, we could leave off the wrapper by adding `--bare` (or `-b` for short).

We'd still have our ordering issue, though. But if we used individual JavaScript files instead of joining the files into one **main.js** file, it would then be up to us to include these output scripts in the HTML page, and we could do that in any order we liked:

```
coffee -b -w -c .
```

Compiling a List of Files

If you dislike the idea of adding a huge stack of JavaScript includes, and you're on a Unix-like system, you could turn to a command line solution. Create a simple text file (which we'll call **files**) that contains each file you want (including relative path), separated by line breaks:

chapter03/src/files

```
gfx.coffee
game.coffee
```

Then perform the compilation by streaming the file paths into `coffee`:

```
xargs -t coffee -j ../script/main.js -w -c < files
```

It's also fairly simple to turn this idea into a small bash script (we'll call it **compile**) and execute that:

chapter03/src/compile

```
#!/bin/sh

xargs -t coffee -j ../script/main.js -w -c << EOF
gfx.coffee
game.coffee
EOF
```

If you set the execute permission (`chmod +x compile`), you can then run it by typing `./compile` (once you have all your files in place).

Keeping Orderly and Up to Date

Remember to add to this list whenever you create a new **.coffee** file. This way, compiling the project will be trivial as you follow along with the examples. Keep in mind that the order they're listed in is important, and that **game.coffee** should always be the last item.

Getting Serious with Cake

Eventually, you'll hit a project that outgrows these simple solutions and needs some more heavy-duty control over the build process. The CoffeeScript installation process included a command called `Cake`. `Cake` is a simple build tool similar in functionality to `Make`[1] or `Rake`[2] (see what they did there?) that automates the process of compiling, building, minifying, and concatenating your CoffeeScript projects. Tasks are defined in a Cakefile and executed when you run the command `cake`. Cakefiles are written in CoffeeScript, so they can be as basic or complex as you need:

```
task 'greet', 'Say hello to everyone', ->
  console.log 'Hello, World!'
```

You can interact with the file system and command line (necessary for running the `coffee` compiler, for example), and completely define your build and deployment process. To learn more about `Cake` and Cakefiles, head over to the wiki.[3]

Handling Player Input

A game is only a game if the user has some input into what's happening, hence our need to handle input. Our game is going to be primarily controlled with the keyboard, so we'll need to hook into the DOM events that fire keyboard events. This is a familiar task in web development, because the Web uses an event-driven model: the user clicks an element, or scrolls a page, or presses a key. Your code listens for these events and responds appropriately.

But games are a little different. Typically a game is driven by a game loop that runs many times a second, and changes are made little by little in each frame to give the appearance of smooth motion. Instead of reacting to events, we want to poll the status of our input devices.

We're using the browser DOM, so we still need to trap the keyboard events when they happen; however, we'll store the state of the keyboard in our `keys` object and interrogate this proxy in the game. We'll also add a field for each key used. While

---

[1] http://linux.101hacks.com/unix/make/

[2] http://guides.rubyonrails.org/command_line.html#rake

[3] https://github.com/jashkenas/coffee-script/wiki/%5BHowTo%5D-Compiling-and-Setting-Up-Build-Tools

we're still yet to know exactly what's happening in our game (thanks very much, lazy team members), we can assume we'll need keys for moving up, down, left, and right, as well as a key for performing an action, such as a fire button. We'll make that the space bar for now, but we can update it later if necessary:

chapter03/src/keys.coffee *(excerpt)*

```
keys =
  up: false,
  down: false,
  left: false,
  right: false,
  space: false,

  reset: ->
    @up = @down = @left = @right = @space = false

  trigger: (keyCode, isDown) -> # handle the key event
```

The properties all default to `false`, which means that they're not pressed. While a key is held down, the value will change to `true`; that way, we can use it as a condition in our game:

```
fire() if keys.space
```

There's also a `reset` function to move everything back to the defaults. It'll come in handy for the times where keys become stuck because keyboard events fail to be sent as expected. For example, the user could press the space bar, then click on a different browser tab, *then* release the key, and finally come back to the game. Because we never receive the `keyup` event, our game still thinks the space bar is being held down.

We'll tie the DOM events to the `keys` object via the `trigger` method. At the bottom of **keys.coffee**—outside of the `keys` object—add the following event handlers:

chapter03/src/keys.coffee *(excerpt)*

```
document.addEventListener "keydown", (e) ->
  keys.trigger e.keyCode, true
, false
```

```
document.addEventListener "keyup", (e) ->
  keys.trigger e.keyCode, false
, false
```

The `document.addEventListener` function allows us to listen for various events. We want the `keydown` and `keyup` events. From these, we extract the `keyCode` (the number associated with each key) and send it off to our `trigger` function, along with a flag indicating whether it was key press or a key release.

DOM Event Listeners

The `addEventListener` is a standard event on modern web browsers—but modern web browsers vary! We can easily write some code that works consistently across browsers, but we're currently in the prototyping phase of our game and need to work quickly. We'll probably replace these calls later with their jQuery equivalent, which takes care of the inconsistencies for us.

Dispatching with Switch

With the events firing correctly and providing us with the key code and key state, we can dispatch this information to our `keys` state. We could do this with a stack of `if` statements that test if each key we care about has been pressed, but a cleaner way is to use the `switch` statement:

chapter03/src/keys.coffee (excerpt)

```
trigger: (keyCode, isDown) ->
  switch keyCode
    when 37 then @left = isDown
    when 39 then @right = isDown
    when 38 then @up = isDown
    when 40 then @down = isDown
    when 32
      console.log "FIRE AWAY!" if isDown
      @space = isDown
```

The key code that the DOM event gives us is an integer representing the key. If we press the right arrow key, the key code will be 37, so we set the `@right` property accordingly.

Where can we find the key codes?

Obviously, resources exist that list all the ASCII standard keys and their codes, but the easiest way is to just add `console.log keyCode` to the `trigger` function and press some keys!

I'm sure you won't be surprised to learn that a `switch` statement is yet another expression that returns a value. This means that it can be assigned directly to a variable, or returned from a function.

Adding the Professor

What's the use of having a godlike ability to form levels if there's no one around to admire our handiwork? We're reaching the end of Day 3 of the Game Jam, so we'd better launch Professor Digman-Rünner into his own game.

Create a new file, **player.coffee**, (remember to add it to your **compile** file) and define a `player` with these properties:

chapter03/src/player.coffee *(excerpt)*

```
player =
  x: gfx.tileW * 3
  y: gfx.tileH * 5
  speed: 4
```

We'll set the Professor at a beginning position of four tiles in and six down, and give him a speed of four (why four? Why not?). Next up, we add two methods: one to `update` the player's position and another to `render` the player:

chapter03/src/player.coffee *(excerpt)*

```
update: ->
render: (gfx) ->
```

These two methods will feature in just about every entity and item we add to our game. The `update` method will update the object's internal state, and the `render` method will represent that state for the current frame. The Professor's `update` method is controlled by looking at the current state of the `keys` object:

```
                                    chapter03/src/player.coffee (excerpt)

update: ->
  @x -= @speed if keys.left
  @x += @speed if keys.right
  @y += @speed if keys.down
  @y -= @speed if keys.up
```

In contrast, when our ninjas are added, they'll have some AI that updates their positions and dictates their actions rather than keyboard input. By now, the render method will be obvious:

```
                                    chapter03/src/player.coffee (excerpt)

render: (gfx) -> gfx.drawSprite 0, 0, @x, @y
```

All we need to do now is call our player's update and render methods. It needs to occur quickly to give the illusion of movement; this is known as the game loop, and will be the subject of the section called "The Game Loop" in Chapter 4. We can do a quick 'n' easy one right now so that you can show those teammates.

In the main game code, after the graphics have been initialized and the level created, we'll add a call to JavaScript's setInterval; this is a function that repeatedly calls some code at a set interval. Sounds perfect for us:

```
                                    chapter03/src/game.coffee (excerpt)

level = makeLevel level1

setInterval ->
  # run game things
  # draw the level
  ⋮
, 33
```

The code will be run every 33 milliseconds. What do we have to run, though? First, we should call our player's update method. Then we can begin rendering, making sure to gfx.clear() before we draw the level, then the player. The setInterval will run its magic and loop through the code again, and again, and again:

chapter03/src/game.coffee *(excerpt)*

```coffee
# run game things
player.update()

gfx.clear()

# draw the level
for row, y in level
  for tile, x in row
    continue if not tile
    xPos = x * gfx.tileW
    yPos = y * gfx.tileH
    gfx.drawSprite tile[0], tile[1], xPos, yPos

player.render(gfx)
```

This gives the illusion of movement. Sort of. The Professor, seen in Figure 3.4, can apparently jetpack around the screen like a bird as we control him with the keyboard. He's yet to interact with the environment, but at least he's alive!

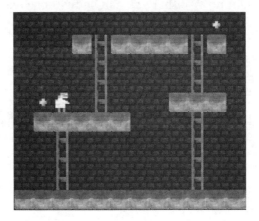

Figure 3.4. Alive and flying

And There Was Light!

What a blast! You were able to learn and use some of the more advanced features of CoffeeScript to implement game levels and a controllable player. More importantly, you have a solid base to build on and an understanding of ideas and goals behind CoffeeScript itself. Now we can apply these ideas and bring our project to life.

Game Loop and Classes

It's now day 4 of 7 and you're starting to sweat. The story writer announced he has too much "real" work on and will have to bow out of the race, but says he still wants a cut of any profits arising from his contributions to the project. You explain to him how percentages of zero work, and he leaves in a huff.

You know that if you lack a solid base to build on by the end of the day, pushing a complete product out the door will be tough. Let's knuckle down and apply some structure to our game. In this chapter, we'll take the prototype we've been working on and refactor it into a bunch of classes that will organize and drive the game.

The Game Loop

But first, we need to clean up our mess from last night. In our haste to put some animation on the screen, we used the simple `setInterval` timer to continually loop over the updating and drawing methods. This morning, we'll need to rework this into what will become the very heart of our game: the game loop.

Unlike the event-driven nature of the Web, a game loop approach requires constant work for the browser: clearing the screen, updating all models, and rendering any changes to the screen. Such operations need to be at least 30 frames per second, otherwise animation will look jumpy. External events, such as user input, are polled by the system every frame, rather than being told to us directly.

Improving Our Loop

It's time to sketch out the `game` module that will be the master of our game universe. We will build on the concepts we developed in previous chapters using new code. It will be responsible for the high-level aspects of the entire game: starting, stopping, resetting, initializing, and scheduling the updates and renders of every object. Here it is stubbed out, so we can fill it in method by method:

chapter04/src/game.coffee

```coffee
@game =
  running: false
  init: ->
  stop: ->
  start: ->
  reset: ->
  tick: ->
  update: ->
  render: ->
```

While we're at it, we should move the call to `game.init` into index.html:

chapter04/index.html (excerpt)

```html
<script src="script/main.js" type="text/javascript"></script>
<script type="text/javascript">game.init()</script>
```

Starting from the top, the `running` flag will be used to start and stop the game, in case we want to add a pause feature at some point. Next up, we have the initialization code, which should look familiar by now:

chapter04/src/game.coffee (excerpt)

```coffee
init: ->
  if not gfx.init()
    alert "Sorry, no canvas"
    return
  gfx.load -> game.reset()
```

Once the `canvas` element has been initialized, the code will call the game's `reset` method. When making a game, it's important to split up your initialization code (which runs just once—at start up) from your reset code (which runs every time the player dies and wants to play again). It's common to bundle all this together when you're prototyping, but it's always a pain to split up later!

 self Reflection

In the callback, we're explicitly referring to the `game` object rather than the `this` object; that's because the code's scope has been altered. There are other ways to get around this; a common one is to keep a reference to the original scope by assigning it to a variable `self = this`, then in the callback using the stored scope `self.reset()`. CoffeeScript also provides us with a nicer approach: function binding, which we'll see in the section called "Function Binding" in Chapter 6.

The `start` and `stop` methods only toggle our internal `running` flag. We could set the field directly, rather than use the setter methods, but later we might want to do some extra logic when a game is paused or resumed:

chapter04/src/game.coffee (excerpt)

```
stop: -> @running = false
start: -> @running = true
```

Our `reset` method is called from the initialization code and will pass on the message to the `keys` object; this ensures there are no key presses stuck from the previous run. It then kicks everything off, setting the `running` property to `true` via `@start()` and calling the main `tick` method. `tick` *is* our game loop—each tick is a frame in our game. It makes sure the timing is correct and fires off the game logic:

chapter04/src/game.coffee (excerpt)

```
reset: ->
  keys.reset()
  if not @running
    @start()
    @tick()
```

In Chapter 3, we used `setInterval` to loop infinitely. The next step up from this is to use its partner in crime, `setTimeout`. `setTimeout` works exactly the same, but it loops just a single time, giving us control over when to do the next tick:

chapter04/src/game.coffee *(excerpt)*

```
tick: ->
  return if not @running
  gfx.clear()
  @update()
  @render()
  setTimeout (-> game.tick()), 33
```

We check that the game is running, and if it is we call the `update` and `render` functions (which we'll define in a while). `setTimeout` is then called, delaying for 33 milliseconds. Why 33? Because that will give us a frame rate of around 30 frames per second. It's derived from the simple calculation: `1000 milliseconds (in a second) / 30 frames = 33`-ish. For most games, modern computers will not flinch at this rate, so you can bump it up if you want. A setting of 16 milliseconds will give you around 60 frames per second (the generally accepted "good" frame rate)—just be sure to test it on the worst computer you want your game to run on!

Looping with `RequestAnimationFrame`

But our game loop is still very naive. Indeed, game loop logic can become extremely complex if you want rock-solid, flawless timing. The core of the problem is that although `setTimeout` says it will call our code after 33 milliseconds, it's prone to being wrong. Sometimes it's a bit slower; sometimes a bit faster; sometimes the browser's garbage collection kicks in and the loop seems to hang for a frame; sometimes, your user will have a slow computer that fails to keep up.

A good game loop will account for all these situations and update accordingly by tying your animation to the `delta` of time that passed since the last tick. You can then move the onscreen entities more or less to make up for lags and hiccups, so that everything appears to move smoothly, all the time. A good game loop will also separate the game logic from the rendering aspects of the code—either by using two distinct looping mechanisms, or via a scheduler inside the main loop. It typically performs rendering as fast as it can, while updating intensive game logic at a slower rate. It will skip frames, or run update logic multiple times in a single loop to keep behavior and presentation synced up.

Good game loops are hard, so we'll resist going down that path. But we can do better than `setTimeout` without breaking our brains, thanks to the recently introduced `requestAnimationFrame` timer.

The `requestAnimationFrame` timer is designed especially for animations,[1] providing us with a smoother experience than its other JavaScript timing brethren. It also has the added advantage of pausing when the user switches tabs, so your game won't be responsible for draining the life out of users' laptops if they forget they've left it open in another tab! The use of the timer is similar to `setTimeout`. In fact, we can just replace the `setTimeout` call directly:

```
requestAnimationFrame ->
  game.tick()
```

We've gained the support of the browser's low-level animation timing mechanisms. One element we've lost, however, is the ability to set the frame rate manually. Everything will be running at 60 frames per second.

This is perfect for our game, but what happens in a few years if the browser vendors decide to bump that speed up, or even down? Our game will be tied to this timer and everything will run much faster or slower.

You can see it's a much smarter idea to keep your animation amounts independent of the frame rate. We'll skip doing this for simplicity's sake, but it's relatively easy to do. A couple of great online resources on the subject are CreativeJS's "The Secret to Silky Smooth JavaScript Animation"[2] and Glen Fiedler's *"Fix Your Timestep."*[3]

Classes

Our primary unit of code reuse till now has been the module: we have a module for the graphics, one for player input, one for the main game object, and one for the player. These have all been (kind of) singletons, meaning that we only have a single

---

[1] https://developer.mozilla.org/en-US/docs/DOM/window.requestAnimationFrame

[2] http://creativejs.com/resources/requestanimationframe/

[3] http://gafferongames.com/game-physics/fix-your-timestep/

instance of each object. It is possible that we'll want more than one instance of the player object (if we make a two-player version), and we'll most surely want more than one ninja attacking the Professor. Additionally, there are a lot of similarities between the Professor and the ninjas that we'd like to extract and reuse.

JavaScript has a model of **prototypal inheritance** for instantiating and extending objects. In this model, our instances are created in a factory-like approach from a prototype function. All instances share the same prototype, meaning that they all have the same methods and properties even when they're added to the prototype *after* instantiation. Although quite different from the classic object-oriented approach, it's very flexible and powerful. So flexible, in fact, that it actually allows us to implement a object-oriented model on top of it—though the syntax required to do so is a little funky. CoffeeScript circumvents the funk by providing some nice syntactic sugar for simple classes.

Classes are defined using the `class` keyword. The smallest class we could create (without properties or methods) consists of the keyword and class name:

```
class Player
```

Under the covers, this will become a regular `function` (called `Player`) that is the prototype function for instantiating our objects. Although the compiled code will look quite different, refactoring our original `player` object into a class is very easy. Our original looked like this:

```
player =
  speed: 4
  update: -> …
  render: (gfx) -> …
```

The x and y properties are gone (for the moment) because they'll need to be set on an instance-by-instance basis, rather than hardcoded. The class version needs only a small modification to its definition to complete the transformation: `class Player`:

chapter04/src/Player.coffee *(excerpt)*

```coffee
class Player
  speed: 4
  update: -> …
  render: (gfx) -> …
```

We changed the name to `Player` with an uppercase P. Uppercasing class names is a common convention, but not vital. If you look at the compiled JavaScript for the class, you'll see that `Player` is no longer an object but a function with the class details attached to its `prototype` property. We can make some players with it using `new`:

```coffee
player1 = new Player()
player2 = new Player()
```

Because each instance is just an object, our player code will continue to work. Each instance has its own properties and methods (the methods being shared among all instances to save memory) that you can set and call:

```coffee
player1.update()
player1.render gfx
player2.speed = 5
```

CoffeeScript's classes are quite simple, and a great way to group related reusable functionality—especially for a game. We'll be using them extensively.

Constructor and Auto Properties

We'll often want to set some parameters or run some startup code for each instance of an object we create. For this, CoffeeScript gives us a special method **constructor** that will be called upon object instantiation:

chapter04/src/Player.coffee *(excerpt)*

```coffee
class Player
  constructor: -> #runs when instantiated
```

Like any function, the constructor can also accept parameters. The most common use of this is to set some initial properties for the instance. We removed the player's x and y coordinates earlier; these would work nicely here, as we'll probably have no idea where we want the player to start until we create it:

chapter04/src/Player.coffee *(excerpt)*

```
constructor: (x, y) ->
  @x = x
  @y = y
```

Just as with ordinary objects, we set class properties using the this alias @. The constructor will assign the parameters we pass in to the class's x and y properties. Doing initialization code like this is so common that CoffeeScript gives us a bit of sugar to make matters cleaner:

chapter04/src/Player.coffee *(excerpt)*

```
constructor: (@x, @y) ->
```

No need to clutter up our constructors with boring details—CoffeeScript can automatically do the boilerplate stuff for us!

 this Is It

Automatically assigning values to this properties is not restricted to classes; you can use it on regular objects, and even functions. The effect is the same, where it assigns the parameter to a property of the same name in the current scope.

When we create our player object, we can now set the screen position dynamically:

```
professor = new Player 10, 20
console.log professor.x, professor.y # ==> 10, 20
```

Class Inheritance

The Professor must be feeling a bit lonely. It's about time we unleashed some hoards of pixel ninjas. These will be encapsulated in a new class (in a file called **Ninja.coffee**) that will contain our ninja logic:

```
                                      chapter04/src/Ninja.coffee (excerpt)

class Ninja
  speed: 4
  update: ->
  render: (gfx) ->
```

Hmm, that looks comparable to the Professor's class definition … and it's likely we'll want to add some more characters later that will be similar too. We could just copy/paste our code, but then if we make any changes, we'd have to modify it everywhere. A better solution is to extract all the similarities into a **base class** and give that functionality to anyone who needs it via **inheritance**: our player and ninjas objects will *inherit* the properties and methods from its parent.

We'll give our generic base character a suitably generic name: `Entity`. Our professor is an `Entity` and each ninja is an `Entity`. Because there will be multiple related objects, we'll make a new subdirectory in our project called **entities** and move **Player.coffee** and **Ninja.coffee** there.

A new file, **_Entity.coffee**, will contain the underlying characteristics that define entities in our game. What you include here will vary from game to game, but some are standard: positions, directions, generic update methods, and so forth:

```
                               chapter04/src/entities/_Entity.coffee (excerpt)

class Entity
  speed: 4
  dir: "LEFT"
  constructor: (@x, @y) ->
  update: ->
  render: (gfx) -> gfx.ctx.fillText "?", @x, @y
```

We've added a new `dir` property to hold the direction that the entity faces (we'll keep it simple by using strings to define either `"LEFT"` or `"RIGHT"`). The constructor will set the x and y properties for us, and the `render` method will draw a question mark at the entity's current location when called.

Why draw a question mark? Well, we'll probably never directly make an `entity` object; rather, we'll call the subclass that inherit from it. Each subclass will override the `render` method with its own implementation (and draw itself correctly). If a subclass forgets to do this, we'll see a question mark appear on the screen and (surely) realize what's going on!

 OOPs!

CoffeeScript's classes aren't intended to replicate a fully blown object-oriented model, so we're unable to make abstract classes or define private variables, although there are ways to replicate these kinds of features (such as wrapping private code in an internal function). This is a consequence of JavaScript's inheritance model, which encourages a functional programming style. Trying to code JavaScript too much like Java will only leave you with leaky abstractions and a bad headache.

With the core entity model defined, we can refactor our Professor and the ninjas to use it. To inherit from a base class, you use the CoffeeScript keyword `extends` followed by the base class name:

chapter04/src/entities/Player.coffee *(excerpt)*

```
class Player extends Entity
  update: -> …
  render: (gfx) -> gfx.drawSprite 0, 0, @x, @y
```

Now the `Player` object has all the features of `Entity`. We've provided a new `render` method that completely shadows the base, so any call to `render` will draw the professor frame instead of the question mark. Refactoring our ninjas is just as easy, and our final `Ninja` class becomes equally small:

chapter04/src/entities/Ninja.coffee *(excerpt)*

```
class Ninja extends Entity
  render: (gfx) -> gfx.drawSprite 0, 1, @x, @y
```

Everything that's the same about a player and a ninja (it turns out that professors and ninjas have a lot in common) is kept neatly in the base class, and anything that differs (currently the visual representation only) is defined in the subclass. Both the base and subclasses will grow substantially bigger before the game is done!

We are now free to freshly mint all the professors and ninjas we need:

```
player = new Player 50, 50
ninja1 = new Ninja 80, 50
player.render gfx
ninja1.render gfx
```

Here's the result in Figure 4.1.

Figure 4.1. The ninja and the Professor

Game Classes

CoffeeScript's classes look like the way to go for our game: they group logic together properly and allow us to easily create armies of ninjas. It's time to really start thinking about what we need in this game in addition to the Professor and ninjas. We are making a tile-based game that will be divided into levels. Each level will be progressively harder, and slowly introduce the player to all the rules of the game.

This means we have to model the levels, and the levels will comprise blocks. The blocks will be the interesting part of our game in that they'll define how our entities move and what they can do. We've been calling them tiles so far; the difference is that a block will be the object containing logic, whereas a tile is simply the image that represents a block.

Later on we'll probably also need some menus and game screens, and maybe even some more classes for any crazy effects we want to add at the end. For now, let's start with the levels.

The Level Class

The level function we created in Chapter 3 was great for putting some pixels on the screen, but we need a bit more control. We'll replace our makeLevel function with a new class, Level. And although it's unnecessary to subclass a level like we did with our entities, we'll nevertheless put it in its own directory—**levels**—because we'll keep our level data in there too.

The primary function of the `Level` class will be to parse our level data and create the blocks. Every time we begin a game, or the player completes a level, we'll create a new `Level` instance and pass in the data to have it load. There are a few properties we'll need to keep track of, too: the `width` and `height` (in tiles) of the level, how many magic particles (which we'll generically call `treasures`) the Professor needs to collect to finish the level, and a list of all the ninjas on the loose:

chapter04/src/levels/Level.coffee *(excerpt)*

```coffee
class Level
  w: 0
  h: 0
  treasures: 0
  ninjas: []
  constructor: (level, @game) -> @load level
  load: (level) ->
  update: ->
  render: (gfx) ->
```

The constructor simply stores a reference to `game` and flips the level data over to the `load` function to do the parsing. We can also see the familiar `update` and `render` methods that will be responsible for updating and rendering all the items the level is managing. We'll leave the `Level` class at stubs for now and fill it out later; we just need to define it so that our entities know about its existence.

Calling the Super Class

Each of our `entity` subclasses has their own `render` method; if we fail to supply one, we have the base class functionality instead. But sometimes you want both the base class functionality and some custom functionality. To achieve this, we use `super` (as in "super class"—not just because it's a great feature) from the subclass.

To see it in action, consider this addition to our game: our entities knowing some facts about the level that they live in. For example, the Professor will have to check what kind of block he's currently standing on to see whether it obstructs his path, or if he's allowed to pass through it. We'll pass the level itself to each entity as we create the entity, and keep a reference for when the level's needed:

chapter04/src/entities/_Entity.coffee *(excerpt)*

```coffee
class Entity
  ⋮
  constructor: (@level, @x, @y) ->
```

The `level` is set, along with the `x` and locations of all of our entities. But now we've decided that we want to personalize the Professor a bit, by changing his default direction. In the base class, we default to `"LEFT"`, but our players will start in the top-left side of the screen; as a consequence, they'll be facing the wrong way.

We'll want to set this inside the `Player` constructor function. But wait! If we put a constructor in the subclass, it will override the base class—and our base properties will fail to be set. Luckily, we can still reach the base class using `super`. `super` will call the base class method of the same name that we're currently in. To put our parameters back up to the `Entity` class, we call `super` inside the constructor:

chapter04/src/entities/Player.coffee *(excerpt)*

```coffee
constructor: (level, x, y) ->
  super level, x, y
  @dir = "RIGHT"
```

This sets the parameters as before, and we can then proceed with our player-specific logic (in this case, it's setting the direction to `"RIGHT"`). That's exactly what we want—although it's a mild inconvenience to have to copy all the function parameters manually like this, as they're exactly the same in the base class. Of course, Coffee-Script gives us some sugar:

chapter04/src/entities/Player.coffee *(excerpt)*

```coffee
constructor: ->
  super
  @dir = "RIGHT"
```

If you call `super` without arguments or parentheses, it will pass *all* parameters directly to the base class. Super! And `super` isn't just for the constructor: any method in a subclass can call the super class's method of the same name. For example, to reuse the base `render` code, we could call it from our `Player` class:

```
render: (gfx) ->
  super
  gfx.drawSprite 0, 0, @x, @y
```

However, if you were to call this in our main game loop, you'd see that only the Professor is drawn, rather than the question mark that we used as our placeholder. Actually, both are called, but the base is called first and the Professor is drawn over the top of it. If we wanted to switch the order, we simply call super after we draw:

```
render: (gfx) ->
  gfx.drawSprite 0, 0, @x, @y
  super
```

If you then hide the background tiles, you'll see the question mark.

No base class?

CoffeeScript implements the super functionality by keeping a reference to the parent class's prototype. When you use super, it simply tries to call the method on the parent prototype—so it's not going to stop you calling a base class method that doesn't exist!

The Block Class

Every tile in our map will be an object, even the blank spaces. This allows us to put a lot of logic into our maps; some blocks will be solid (and impossible to walk through), some will be diggable (in order to dig holes), and some will be climbable (so that we can have ladders for our entities to go up and down). We'll put each block in its own class, but derive them from a common base class called Block, which will live in the file, **_Block.coffee**, in a new directory: **blocks**!

chapter04/src/blocks/_Block.coffee (excerpt)

```
class Block
  solid: false
  constructor: ->
  update: ->
  render: (gfx, x, y) ->
```

Extending Prototypes

If you weren't using CoffeeScript's class helpers and wanted to add methods to the object's prototype directly, you can use the extends operator, `::`. For example, `Block::update` is the equivalent of `Block.prototype.update`.

Like our entities, blocks will have an `update` and a `render` method that will be called every frame. Unlike our entities, blocks will lack their own position—the `Level` class will send the `x` and `y` tile locations along when it calls the `render` function. Because we're doing nothing inside the block's `render` function, this block will be invisible.

So while we're here, let's define our first visible block: `Dirt`. Dirt will be one of our primary platform materials. The entities will be unable to walk on or fall through dirt, but the Professor will be able to dig into it later:

chapter04/src/blocks/Dirt.coffee (excerpt)

```
class Dirt extends Block
  solid: true
  render: (gfx, x, y) -> gfx.drawSprite 4, 1, x, y
```

`Dirt` extends our base `Block` class but overrides the `solid` property (our flag for disallowing entities to pass) and `render` to draw the correct tile for this block:

chapter04/src/game.coffee (excerpt)

```
d = new Dirt()
d.render gfx, 10, 10
```

Our block, shown in Figure 4.2, is relatively unexciting, but it has potential. And adding new blocks with any crazy functionality you can imagine becomes easy.

Figure 4.2. Uneventful block

Loading Levels

With all our classes in place, we can start to thread everything together. In Chapter 3, we took a stab at drawing a map of tiles; now, we're going to refactor that into more heavyweight code. First, we add a file—**levels.coffee**—in the **levels** directory that will hold the definition of all our game levels:

chapter04/src/levels/levels.coffee *(excerpt)*

```
levels = [{
  name: "DIG and BUILD"
  data: """
    .P...............X.....
    @-@@.........@@@@@@@-@..
    .#..@@@..............#...
    .#.....@@.@@.....X..#...
    @OO#.........#@@...O#..^
    ...#..........#.....#.^O
    ...#..@@-@@@@#..-@@@@@OO
    ...#....#....#..#......
    ...#....#....#..#......
    ...#....#....#..#......
    @-@@OOOOO.#.@@@@@#@@-@@@
    .#.X.......#......#..#...
    .#...*.....#......#..#...
    ####..@@#@@..-@@@@@@@..*
    ####....#....#.........#
    ####....#....#.........#
    OOOOOOOOOOOOOOOOOOOOOOOO
  """}]
```

This will be an array of objects. Each object will be a level containing a name (which we'll eventually display before the level commences), a multiline string data that plots the level map as we did earlier. Our Level only understands a few symbols so far: "." for a blank block, and @ for a dirt block. Shortly, we'll add X for a ninja, and P for the Professor. We're going to ignore the Professor for the time being—he's a special case that we'll look at shortly—but we'll place him in the level map because it would be rude to omit him.

Defining our ninjas and players inside our map like this is cheating a bit; a ninja is not a block, it's an entity. When our level loader encounters an X, it needs to do a few tasks to introduce a new ninja properly. We'll pull these out into a small helper function inside `Level`:

```
                                    chapter04/src/levels/Level.coffee (excerpt)
load: (level) ->
addNinja: (x, y) ->
  xPos = x  * gfx.tileW
  yPos = y  * gfx.tileH ❶
  ninja = new Ninja @, xPos, yPos ❷
  @ninjas.push ninja ❸
```

❶ First, it has to calculate the screen pixel position of the ninja from the provided map position.

❷ It then creates a new instance of our `Ninja` class (passing the level instance, and the screen x and y location).

❸ Finally, the ninja is added to the level's array of ninjas so that we can wrangle them as a group.

Test this method by manually adding a ninja from inside the `Level` constructor:

```
@addNinja 1, 1
ninja = @ninjas[0]
alert "Ninja 1 at: #{ninja.x}, #{ninja.y}"
```

Now we can revisit our level-loading magic. Here are the steps to transform our ASCII art into the level model:

```
                                    chapter04/src/levels/Level.coffee (excerpt)
load: (level) ->
  # 1. Clear level items
  # 2. Parse the level string into a map
  # 3. Loop over the map and create the blocks
  # 4. Set the level height and width
```

Step one is nice and easy; each time we begin a level (whether it's a new game, a new level, or the player has died and is restarting), we need to ensure that the correct state is reset. We remove any ninjas that we've already created, and set the `treasure` count back to 0:

```
                                    chapter04/src/levels/Level.coffee (excerpt)

# 1. Clear level items
@ninjas = []
@treasures = 0
```

Next up is to parse the level `data` string. This uses exactly the same `for` comprehension that we used originally to turn the string into a 2D array of characters:

```
                                    chapter04/src/levels/Level.coffee (excerpt)

# 2. Parse the level string into a map
asciiMap = (row.split "" for row in level.data.split "\n")
```

When the Parentheses Count

The parentheses in this statement are a prerequisite. If you omit them, the loop results won't be collated into an array—you'll just have the value of the final expression.

Here comes the fun part: making some real blocks. The plan is to loop over the `asciiMap` we just created and map each character symbol to its corresponding `Block` instance. The result will be a 2D array that's the same size as `asciiMap`, except populated with blocks:

```
                                    chapter04/src/levels/Level.coffee (excerpt)

# 3. Loop over the map and create the blocks
@map = for row, y in asciiMap
  for col, x in row
    switch col
      when "@" then new Dirt()
      when "X"
        @addNinja x, y
        new Block()
      else new Block()
```

Remember that the `switch` statement can return a value, so we make sure to return some kind of `Block` for every possible case. If we find a `@`, we return a new `Dirt` object; if we find an `X`, we add a new `Ninja` via our helper method and return an empty block. And if we find an unknown symbol (which will be the "."s and the Professor's P in our map), we return an empty block.

Cheats Never Prosper

Earlier, we said that defining the ninjas in the ASCII map was cheating. Here's why. When we find an entity, we instantiate and process it, then *replace it with an empty block*. That means entities can only *ever* start on an empty block. A better solution is to declare separate maps for entities and blocks, and process them separately. The downside to this approach is that it's difficult to see at a glance everything in your level.

The final step is to set a couple of helpful level properties: h (the height) and w (the width) of the newly processed map:

chapter04/src/levels/Level.coffee (excerpt)

```
# 4. Set the level height and width
@h = @map.length
@w = @map[0].length
```

To use the load method, pass in the level we want to use (we only made a single level, so can only use level[0] for now). To test it, create a new Level from outside:

```
myLevel = new Level levels[0]
```

We end up with our map property populated properly and some ninjas neatly nested in the ninjas array. A lot of alliteration, but little fun—because we see nothing yet.

Driving a Level

Now that we've modeled a level, how can we use it in the game? Once again, it's back to our trusty update and render methods. Unlike an entity or a block, the level is no screen object; as a result, it does no internal processing of its own, but rather manages the child items it's responsible for: the ninjas and the map blocks:

```
                                chapter04/src/levels/Level.coffee (excerpt)
update: ->
  # Update the level blocks
  for row in @map
    for block in row
      block.update()
  ninjas.update() for ninjas in @ninjas
```

Every block receives an update notice, even though nobody needs it at the moment; they will soon enough. For example, the `Dirt` block can be dug away, but it will reappear over time; the `update` method is where we'll perform this kind of logic. The ninjas all receive the update message too; this is where we'll perform our AI calculations for attacking the Professor.

All that's left is to display the level to the user. This is almost identical to updating, but passes in x and y tile coordinates for rendering at the right place on the screen:

```
                                chapter04/src/levels/Level.coffee (excerpt)
render: (gfx) ->
  # Render the level blocks
  for row, y in @map
    for block, x in row
      block.render gfx, x  * gfx.tileW, y  * gfx.tileH
  ninjas.render gfx for ninjas in @ninjas
```

Kicking It All Off

We're still yet to have anything onscreen. Before we address this, let's deal with the glaring omission: the Professor. We added him to the level data map without bringing him to life. Because the Professor will transcend individual levels, we'll define him at the `game` scope and have the level call the code from the game to position him. In the `game` object, add this helper:

```
                                   chapter04/src/game.coffee (excerpt)
setPlayer: (x, y, level) ->
  @player.level = level
  @player.x = x
  @player.y = y
```

This will give the player the current level and set his x and y location. The level then calls this helper when it finds a P in the ASCII map. In the `Level` class, we'll add a method after the `addNinja` method (passing the calculated x and y position and the `this` reference, which is the current level instance):

chapter04/src/levels/Level.coffee *(excerpt)*

```
addPlayer: (x, y) ->
  @game.setPlayer x * gfx.tileW, y * gfx.tileH, @
addNinja: (x, y) ->
```

Then we add a new case to the level loading `switch` statement. It's the same as for the ninja's: adding the player, and returning a new empty block:

chapter04/src/levels/Level.coffee *(excerpt)*

```
when "P"
  @addPlayer x, y
  new Block()
```

One Professor

There's only one professor per map. He's instantiated at the game level, so even if we included multiple Ps in the ASCII map, the `addPlayer` method will reset the player's position, rather than create a new instance as with the ninjas.

The moment has arrived, with all the pieces now in place. At the start of the game `reset` method (which will be called every time the game restarts), create a new `Player` and a new `Level`:

chapter04/src/game.coffee *(excerpt)*

```
reset: ->
  @player = new Player
  @level = new Level levels[0], @
```

We give them a heartbeat by calling `update` and `render` every tick:

```
                                          chapter04/src/game.coffee (excerpt)
update: ->
  @level.update()
  @player.update()
render: ->
  @level.render gfx
  @player.render gfx
```

I hope you can see how the `update` and `render` idea permeates throughout the game. At the top level, we have a game loop that calls our two primary methods. The game is responsible for two children: the `player` and the `level`. In turn, these children can have children of their own. The `level` manages the `ninjas` and the `blocks`, and so passes the heartbeat down to them, as shown in Figure 4.3. In this way, the message filters down to all the objects in the game: "Update yourself. Draw yourself." And there we have the heart of a game.

Figure 4.3. Implanting a heartbeat

Adding New Blocks

Content with the solid foundations you've built for the game, you show the team, outlining the impressive new game loop and extensible class-based system.

"Looks exactly the same as yesterday," says the web technician. "Did you do anything?"

In a bid to prove that your work was not for naught, you make the bold claim that adding new blocks to the game is so simple you can do it in minutes. The team gather incredulously around your laptop.

"First, we need a rock block," you start. "It's just like the dirt block we have, but it will be undiggable and unmovable."

You create a file in the **block** folder called **Rock.coffee**, and extend the `Block` class:

chapter04/src/blocks/Rock.coffee *(excerpt)*

```
class Rock extends Block
  solid: true
  render: (gfx, x, y) -> gfx.drawSprite 4, 0, x, y
```

Next, you add the code to create a new `Rock` instance in the `Level` loading coding:

chapter04/src/levels/Level.coffee *(excerpt)*

```
when "@" then new Dirt()
when "O" then new Rock()
```

"And that's it," you say, a little smugly. "Rocks rock!"

"Hmm," says the pixel artist, unimpressed. "It's just the same as the `Dirt` block. Why don't you add the magic-collectible-particle-thing you've been talking about? And make it move or something."

"Oookaay … " you say, pondering the best way to display the magical "Pig's Boffin" particle. Just like the `Rock`, you create a new class for the particle called **Treasure.coffee**, which, of course, must also extend the `Block` base class.

chapter04/src/blocks/Treasure.coffee *(excerpt)*

```
class Treasure extends Block
  render: (gfx, x, y) ->
    gfx.drawSprite 5, 1, x, y
```

Add `treasures` to the level loading class. There is one difference here: the particles represent the actual *goal* of the level. When all particles are collected, the level is finished, so you need to keep track of how many are around. At the start of the level loading code, you reset the `@treasure` variable to 0. Every time you add a new particle to the game, you have to increment this counter:

chapter04/src/levels/Level.coffee *(excerpt)*

```
when "*"
  @treasures++
  new Treasure()
```

You add a few "*"s to the map and test that the particles are showing up. Good—but there's no movement. Suddenly, you have an idea: how about having the particles "float" up and down by following a small sine wave path? We'll need a state variable to keep track of the offset, so we'll initialize it to a random value between 0 and Pi:

chapter04/src/blocks/Treasure.coffee *(excerpt)*

```
class Treasure extends Block
  constructor: -> @yOff = Math.random() * Math.PI
```

And then update the offset by a small amount every frame. The divisor represents the *frequency* that the particle will oscillate at:

chapter04/src/blocks/Treasure.coffee *(excerpt)*

```
update: -> @yOff +=  Math.PI / 24
```

Now we can add the offset into the rendering code. We take the sine of the offset and multiply it by a constant representing the *amplitude* of the wave:

chapter04/src/blocks/Treasure.coffee *(excerpt)*

```
ySine = Math.floor Math.sin(@yOff) * 4
gfx.drawSprite 5, 1, x, y + ySine
```

"Whoa!" exclaim the team as they witness the action in Figure 4.4. "Awesome!"

Figure 4.4. The bouncing particle over time

Stay Classy

Having comprehended the benefits of splitting up your game into small manageable pieces, you start thinking about the next steps. You now have the base of a game, and a good working knowledge of (nearly) all CoffeeScript's major features. There are a few tricks to learn yet, and so many toys to add to the game, but you now have quiet confidence in CoffeeScript making matters much easier from here on in …

Chapter

Bringing a Game to Life

This chapter is going to apply all that we've learned, rigorously and unrelentingly. We have a long day ahead of us: block collisions, entity collisions, gravity, ladders, AI, collectibles, digging, and building. It seems like a forest of features but, thankfully, our base lets us easily add them one tree at a time.

Block Collision Detection

Our levels are ephemeral at the moment; pretty pictures in the background with no effect on our players. We need some collision detection, as evident in Figure 5.1.

  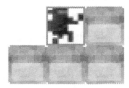

Figure 5.1. Up against the wall

The principle behind our block collision code goes like this: starting from a current picture (the first image in Figure 5.1), the entity will register its intent to move (either through AI for the ninjas, or by pressing the keys for the player). We take this intent and see how many pixels it would move if nothing was blocking it (the second image in Figure 5.1). We test this new position, and if something is blocking the entity, we move it back a little to the correct position so that it's touching the edges of the block, without overlapping it (the final image in Figure 5.1).

This task is made more difficult because at any point the player could be touching several blocks (up to four in our game, because the entities are smaller than the block's width and height). So our pseudo code (which will be in the `_Entity` base class) goes like this:

chapter05/src/entities/_Entity.coffee (excerpt)

```
class Entity
  x: 0
  y: 0
  w: 18
  h: 24
  ⋮
  move: (x, y) ->
    # 1. Determine the intended position we'll move to
    # 2. Check possible block collisions due to vertical movement
    # 3. If collision occurs, move entity back to the edge
    # 4. Check possible block collisions due to horizontal movement
    # 5. If edges overlap, move entity back a little
    # 6. Finally, add the allowed movement to the current position
```

The `move` function accepts the `x` and `y` offsets (the amount we want to move) from the entity's current location. We need to check the vertical amount separately from the horizontal amount because even if one of them is blocked, the other may be free. Checking separately allows our entities to "slide" along walls rather than just stopping dead as soon as they touch a solid block.

Thankfully, steps two and three are almost identical to steps four and five; however, there's still a big chunk of code to complete, and we'll need some helper functions to do so. Define a new file called **_utils.coffee** for holding all our little utility functions that will be used throughout the game:

```
                                     chapter05/src/_utils.coffee (excerpt)
utils =
  now: -> new Date().getTime()
  snap: (value, snapSize) -> Math.floor(value / snapSize) * snapSize
  rand: (min, max) ->
    if not max?
      max = min
      min = 0
    range = max - min
    Math.floor (Math.random() * range) + min
```

They can then be used like so:

```
utils.now()
```

The now function returns the current time in milliseconds, which will be used a lot for animations and general timing. The snap function we'll need for our collision detection; its purpose is to give us the closest grid crossing based on the "snap size." For example, we can find the left edge of a tile by snapping a position to the tile width. Consider our player is at position 50, and our tiles are 24 pixels wide:

```
utils.snap(50, 24) # => 48
```

This tells us that the left edge of the tile the player is in lies at pixel 48—very handy when working with grids. Okay, back to the Entity class. In the move function, we'll first set up a couple of variables:

```
                               chapter05/src/entities/_Entity.coffee (excerpt)
# 1. Determine the intended position we'll move to
xo = x
yo = y
xv = @x + xo
yv = @y + yo
```

We keep a copy of the x and y movements because they'll be updated in the function and we need a reference to the originals. Next, we find the actual screen position the entity will move to by adding the intent to the current location.

To figure out which blocks our entities are touching, we have to look at each corner of the entity and see where it is in relation to the map.

Imagine that our Professor is falling through the air. No blocks are around to stop him. Suddenly (as depicted in Figure 5.2) he meets with the earth. If you asked his top-left, top-right, or bottom-right corners if he could keep falling, they'd say "no problem—our tiles are blank!" However, if you asked his bottom-left corner, it would reply, "Um, no, actually—we're gonna hit dirt if you let us move during this frame!"

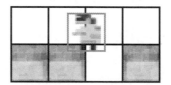

Figure 5.2. On a collision course

To figure out the type of block we'd be touching, we'll add some helpers to the Level source: first, a tool to convert from an (x, y) screen position to the corresponding tile number. This is done by dividing the coordinate values by their respective tile dimensions:

chapter05/src/levels/Level.coffee *(excerpt)*

```
getBlockIndex: (x, y) -> [
  Math.floor x / gfx.tileW
  Math.floor y / gfx.tileH
]
```

If the player is standing at position (30, 10), level.getBlockIndex(30, 10) will return the array [1, 0] corresponding to the map index 1 across and 0 down. We can use this helper to locate the actual map block instance:

chapter05/src/levels/Level.coffee *(excerpt)*

```
getBlock: (x, y) ->
  tiles = @getBlockIndex x, y
  xBlock = tiles[0]
  yBlock = tiles[1]
  @map[yBlock]?[xBlock] or new Rock()
```

If the tile location is invalid, we return a new `Rock` instance that will block the entity's path and avoids them wandering off into the void:

```
level.getBlock(100, 100) # => Rock object
```

Destructured Assignment 1: Arrays

The `getBlock` function works, but it's a bit annoying that we have to unravel the return value of the `getBlockIndex` call into its component pieces using the temporary `tiles` variable. To get around it, CoffeeScript provides a powerful and addictive feature: **destructured assignment** (also often called **pattern matching**—a term I prefer). It lets us pull apart an element, match some (or all) parts of it, and assign the matched pieces to other variables, all in a single statement.

We can use destructured assignment to eliminate the `tile` variable altogether, assigning directly to the `xBlock` and `yBlock` variables:

chapter05/src/levels/Level.coffee *(excerpt)*

```
getBlock: (x, y) ->
  [xBlock, yBlock] = @getBlockIndex x, y
  @map[yBlock]?[xBlock] or new Rock()
```

The format looks a little weird at first, because the left-hand side of the expression is an array! CoffeeScript pulls the result of the right-hand side apart, and assigns the corresponding elements to those on the left-hand side.

We could use this feature for switching the values of variables without using an intermediate variable:

```
[x, y] = [y, x]
```

Pattern matching is fantastically powerful and very expressive. Here's an example of another `Level` helper function that uses our new-found feature in the middle of a `for` comprehension:

chapter05/src/levels/Level.coffee *(excerpt)*

```
getBlocks: (coords) -> @getBlock x, y for [x, y] in coords
```

getBlocks will fetch multiple blocks in one call at once if we provide an array of arrays each containing the (*x*, *y*) position to check. It's useful because our entity has four corners, so we can check them all in a single call. We'll apply it back in our entity's move method as step two of the collision-detection routine:

chapter05/src/entities/_Entity.coffee *(excerpt)*

```
# 2. Check possible block collisions due to vertical movement
[tl, bl, tr, br] = @level.getBlocks([
  [@x, yv],
  [@x, yv + (@h - 1)],
  [@x + (@w - 1), yv],
  [@x + (@w - 1), yv + (@h - 1)]])
```

The getBlocks call will return a Block instance for each of the position arrays we ask for. We're asking for four: the top-left, bottom-left, top-right, and bottom-right coordinates of the entity. Because an array is returned, we can destructure the result into four variables (tl, bl, tr, and br) for further processing. If we applied this call to the Professor's position as depicted back in Figure 5.2, we'd have this result:

```
[Block, Dirt, Block, Block]
```

This indicates that everything is clear except for the bottom-left corner, which is a dirt block.

Mix and Match

Pattern matching is not limited to arrays. If you're feeling the power, stay tuned for the coming sections, where we see a few more tricks up this fantastic feature's sleeves.

As we're only checking vertical movement in this call, we check the entity's current *x* position, and its intended (rather than current) *y* position. To clarify this further, let's break down the fourth position in the array: the bottom-right corner point:

```
@x + (@w - 1), yv + (@h - 1)
```

The bottom-right corner of the entity (checking for vertical movement) is the current x position (@x) plus the entity's width (minus one because it's zero-based), and the intended y position (yv) plus the entity's height (again, minus one).

Before we use the blocks found, we have to add one last helper method to the Level class: a tool to give us the pixel position of the edge of the block we're in. We'll use this to ascertain how much we have to move the player or the ninja back if they try to move into a solid object:

chapter05/src/levels/Level.coffee *(excerpt)*

```
getBlockEdge: (position, forVertical = false) ->
  snapTo = if not forVertical then gfx.tileW else gfx.tileH
  utils.snap position, snapTo
```

This uses the snap utility function we made earlier. If we're checking vertical movement, it will report the top-closest edge; otherwise, it'll return the left-closest edge. The distance between the entity's position and an edge is the number of pixels to shift:

chapter05/src/entities/_Entity.coffee *(excerpt)*

```
# 3. If collision occurs, move entity back to the edge
if y < 0 and (tl.solid or tr.solid)
  yo = @level.getBlockEdge(@y, "VERT") - @y
if y > 0 and (bl.solid or br.solid)
  yo = @level.getBlockEdge(yv + (@h - 1), "VERT") - @y - @h
```

The first if condition will be true if the entity is trying to move upwards, and if the top-left or top-right blocks it will be touching are solid. If so, it gets moved back a little bit to a non-touching position. It does the same again if the player is trying to move downwards, and is blocked by the bottom-left or bottom-right blocks.

Steps 4 and 5 are almost identical to 2 and 3—but we are checking the horizontal changes: that is, we add the intended x movement amount to the current position and see what would happen if we tried to move there. If there is a collision, we update the movement amount until there isn't:

chapter05/src/entities/_Entity.coffee *(excerpt)*

```coffee
# 4. Check possible block collisions due to horizontal movement
[tl, bl, tr, br] = @level.getBlocks([
  [@x, yv],
  [@x, yv + (@h - 1)],
  [@x + (@w - 1), yv],
  [@x + (@w - 1), yv + (@h - 1)]])

# 5. If edges overlap, move entity back a little
if x < 0 and (tl.solid or bl.solid)
  xo = @level.getBlockEdge(@x) - @x
if x > 0 and (tr.solid or br.solid)
  xo = @level.getBlockEdge(xv + (@w - 1)) - @x - @w
```

The results of this armful of code are two carefully calculated variables: xo and yo. These contain the amount the entity is allowed to move in order to avoid colliding. We add these amounts to the entity's position:

chapter05/src/entities/_Entity.coffee *(excerpt)*

```coffee
# 6. Finally, add the allowed movement to the current position
@x += xo
@y += yo
```

Phew. That was fairly complex—though our pattern matching at least lets us write it in a clear way. To place our collision detection into the game, we have to modify our player-handling code. Instead of updating the player's position directly, we keep track of intended movements in some temporary variables, and then pass them to our move function when we want to check for collisions:

chapter05/src/entities/Player.coffee *(excerpt)*

```coffee
update: ->
  xo = yo = 0

  xo -= @speed if keys.left
  xo += @speed if keys.right
  yo += @speed if keys.down
  yo -= @speed if keys.up

  @move(xo, yo)
```

As we fly around the screen, the move function will prevent us from going through solid walls. Suddenly it feels a lot more game-like!

Splats

Before we move on, we'll quickly revisit the getBlocks method, which accepted an array of arrays each containing an (*x*, *y*) position. The extra array wrapper is an unnecessary data structure for this simple check; it would be more natural to accept any number of parameters and apply the getBlock function to each. CoffeeScript gives us a convenient way to carve up our arrays (including function parameter lists) using **splats**, which "soak up" lists of arguments:

chapter05/src/levels/Level.coffee (excerpt)

```
getBlocks: (coords...) -> @getBlock x, y for [x, y] in coords
```

Splatted arguments are written with a trailing ellipsis (...) and indicate that the parameter can contain multiple values. To use this in our original move code, we simply remove the wrapping array and pass each position array as individual parameters:

chapter05/src/levels/Level.coffee (excerpt)

```
[tl, bl, tr, br] = @level.getBlocks(
  [xv, @y],
  [xv, @y + (@h - 1)],
  [xv + (@w - 1), @y],
  [xv + (@w - 1), @y + (@h - 1)])
```

This code will now work equally happily with one or many parameters without requiring the redundant array wrapper.

Splats can be even more powerful than this, though: they don't have to be the first and only parameter of a function. You can specify as many normal parameters as you need and designate one of them to be "the rest." In the following example, we have a function that takes any number of points. The function uses moveTo to move to the first point, and then lineTo to draw lines between the subsequent points:

```
drawLines = (head, tail...) ->
  gfx.ctx.moveTo head.x, head.y
  gfx.ctx.lineTo p.x, p.y for p in tail
```

In this case, splats are great because they allow us to treat the first parameter differ-ently from the rest. Splats can be applied to any array, and they don't have to be located as the final parameter either. In this final example, we chop up the leaderboard array into the first, middle, and last component parts:

```
leaderboard = ["ERC, AMY, BOB, AAA, STU"]

[winner, others..., loser] = leaderboard
console.log """
  First place: #{winner}.
  Last place: #{loser}."""
```

If the leaderboard array contained only two elements, the others parameter would be an empty list. If it fails to contain enough to fill in the fixed parameters of winner and loser, they would be undefined.

Splats and Destructured Assignment

You can also combine splats with a destructured assignment. For example, [first, others..., last] = level.map would assign the first map block to the first variable, the last to last, and everything else to others.

You can have only one splat per list, naturally; if you included more, CoffeeScript would have no way of knowing how you wanted your arguments chopped up!

Gravity

With our solid walls in full effect, we now have quite a good role-playing game shaping up. Unfortunately, we're making a platform game! To rectify this, we need to force some gravity upon our entities. To simulate gravity, we apply a small con-stant downward movement every frame to any entity not standing on solid ground.

We'll have two new flags on our entity objects: one to indicate whether they're falling or not, and a second to indicate if they were falling in the previous frame (this will be useful for doing ninja AI). We initialize them to true so that they're in motion to begin with, and will adjust themselves accordingly in the first frame. Add and initialize the flags in the constructor:

chapter05/src/entities/_Entity.coffee *(excerpt)*

```
constructor: (@level, @x, @y) ->
  # Falling flags
  @falling = true
  @wasFalling = true
```

Now in the move function, right at the beginning, we can add our gravity constant: 2 x entity speed. It might not be the scientifically accurate $9.81m/s^2$—but it looks good enough in action (be sure to play around with it!):

chapter05/src/entities/_Entity.coffee *(excerpt)*

```
move: (x, y) ->
  # Add falling speed
  y += @speed * 2 if @falling
  @wasFalling = @falling
```

Further down the method, when we're checking our vertical downward movement, we have to update the @falling flag to false if we hit a solid bottom-left or bottom-right block:

chapter05/src/entities/_Entity.coffee *(excerpt)*

```
if y > 0 and (bl.solid or br.solid)
  yo = @level.getBlockEdge(yv + (@h - 1), "VERT") - @y - @h
  @falling = false # Add this line to stop falling!
```

We only apply gravity if our entities are falling, which is true when the game initializes, but is set to false when we hit the ground. And it's never set to true ever again—even if our entities walk right out into thin air! We need to ameliorate the move function to do some additional logic based on the blocks our entities are (or aren't) touching. Let's break this logic up into a separate function that runs after we've done the final (x, y) move:

chapter05/src/entities/_Entity.coffee *(excerpt)*

```
# Add the allowed movement
@x += xo
@y += yo

# check the new position!
@checkNewPos x, y
```

The new `checkNewPos` function is passed the original x and y amounts we requested to move. This lets us perform some logic based on the user's intent:

chapter05/src/entities/_Entity.coffee *(excerpt)*

```
checkNewPos: (origX, origY) ->
  # check edges and underfoot
  nearBlocks = [tl, bl, tr, br] = @level.getBlocks(
    [@x, @y],
    [@x, @y + @h],
    [@x + (@w - 1), @y],
    [@x + (@w - 1), @y + @h])
```

We perform a new check on the player's actual position to determine the blocks that are now touching. We've assigned them to individual block variables (`tl`, `bl`, and so on), as well as the `nearBlocks` array containing them all. We'll see why shortly.

Let's now test if an entity has started to fall. This is true if they aren't already falling, and if they aren't standing on the ground. (The call is split into nested `if` statements, because I know we'll be adding some more stuff when we get to ladders!):

chapter05/src/entities/_Entity.coffee *(excerpt)*

```
# Make sure we're standing on solid ground
if not @falling
  if not (bl.solid or br.solid)
    @falling = true
```

And now our entities are falling! There's one final change to make to the player for reasons that are specific to the rules of the game: in our game you're unable to move horizontally while you are falling. This is unusual for platform games (even though it's more realistic!), but we need to prevent the player from reaching platforms we don't want them to, without solving our devious level puzzles.

Inside the `Player` class, add a condition around the left and right key logic:

```
if not @falling
  if keys.left
    xo -= @speed
    @dir = "LEFT"

  if keys.right
    xo += @speed
    @dir = "RIGHT"
```

Ladders

Gravity is great and all, but it's no fun being stuck at the bottom of a level for the whole game. We need some ladders to lift people back up into the air. When an entity is touching a ladder, they can move up or down it to reach other platforms. So, without further ado, let's look at the new block in the game: `Ladder.coffee`:

```
class Ladder extends Block
  climbable: true
  constructor: (@top) ->
    @frame = if top then 6 else 5
  render: (gfx, x, y) -> gfx.drawSprite @frame, 0, x, y
```

There are a couple of special aspects to the ladder. First, it has a `climbable` property, indicating an entity can go up and down it. We have to add this property into the `Block` base class, too, but set it to false, so that no other blocks are accidentally climbable:

```
class Block
  solid: false
  climbable: false
  ⋮
```

Second, we render a different image frame depending on whether we pass `true` or `false` to the constructor's `top` parameter. This is just to render an alternative image for the very top rung of the ladder. To get these guys onto the screen, we add the creation code to our block factory inside **Level.coffee** :

chapter05/src/levels/Level.coffee *(excerpt)*

```coffee
when "#" then new Ladder()
when "-" then new Ladder true # Top of the ladder
```

Ladders are quite complex entities. While they're simple at heart, there are a lot of edge cases we need to consider to make the interaction between player and ladder feel natural. We'll start with the easy parts first. Like with gravity, we'll add some flags to keep track of the entity's state in the `Entity` constructor:

chapter05/src/entities/_Entity.coffee *(excerpt)*

```coffee
# Ladder flags
@onLadder = false
@wasOnLadder = false
@onTopOfLadder = false
```

The interesting one here is `onTopOfLadder`. This needs to be set to `true` when the player is at the very top of a ladder; it's used for the ninja AI, and for stopping a player from moving up into the sky when its feet are touching a ladder, but there is no ladder above it.

To set these flags, we'll employ the `checkNewPos` method:

chapter05/src/entities/_Entity.coffee *(excerpt)*

```coffee
checkNewPos: (origX, origY) ->
  @wasOnLadder = @onLadder
```

We first store the value of the old `onLadder` variable, like we did with gravity. Next, we'll add some code after the block check (where we set the `nearBlocks` array) to perform the core of our ladder logic:

chapter05/src/entities/_Entity.coffee *(excerpt)*

```coffee
# Touching ladder logic
@onLadder = false
touchingALadder = nearBlocks.some (block) -> block.climbable
```

Every frame, we are initializing `onLadder` to `false`. The next line uses the JavaScript `some` function to see if any of the blocks we're touching are climbable. `some` takes an array of elements and returns `true` if at least one of the elements matches the predicate function. In our case, we check all the `nearBlocks` to see if any are climbable:

chapter05/src/entities/_Entity.coffee *(excerpt)*

```coffee
if touchingALadder
  @onLadder = true
  @falling = false

  # Snap to ladders if trying to go up or down
  ⋮
```

If the entity is on a ladder, we have some work to do. We set the `onLadder` property and set `falling` to `false` (you can never be falling if you're touching a ladder!). We also prepare for the big one: snapping our entity to the ladder. If the intent is to move up or down, we'll snap the entity to the center of the ladder. This solves some problems with entities stuck between ladders and blocks, and makes the game feel, well, snappy!

chapter05/src/entities/_Entity.coffee *(excerpt)*

```coffee
# Snap to ladders if trying to go up or down
if origY isnt 0
  snapAmount = utils.snap @x, gfx.tileW
  if not (bl.climbable or tl.climbable)
    @x = snapAmount + gfx.tileW
  if not (br.climbable or tr.climbable)
    @x = snapAmount
```

We only do this if there was intent to move up or down (the `origY` is not zero). If the blocks to the left of the entity are not ladders, we snap to the right by adding one tile's width to the snap amount; if the tiles to the right are not climbable, we snap to the left edge. In Figure 5.3, we can see the Professor climbing towards the top of our recently implemented ladder.

Figure 5.3. Admiring the view

And that's it for touching ladders. But we still have some matters to fix up outside of our `touchingALadder` check. The first concerns standing *on the very top* of a ladder. This is a bit weird, because we have to check that: a) we're on the ladder, b) the blocks above our head are not climbable, and c) the position of our feet (y position + height) is at the very bottom of the tile (the modulus of the feet position in regard to the tile height is 0):

chapter05/src/entities/_Entity.coffee *(excerpt)*

```
@onTopOfLadder =
  @onLadder and not (tl.climbable or tr.climbable) and
  (@y + @h) % gfx.tileH is 0
```

Finally, at the very bottom of the `checkNewPos` function, we can update our "standing on solid ground" test to account for ladders. We do this by adding checks for the `onLadder` flag, and the blocks' `climbable` flag:

chapter05/src/entities/_Entity.coffee *(excerpt)*

```
# Make sure we're standing on solid ground
if not @onLadder and not @falling
  if not (bl.solid or br.solid or bl.climbable or br.climbable)
    @falling = true
```

To restrict the Professor's vertical movement to ladders, we add a couple of tests to the player's `update` function. The player can only move up and down if the up or down key is pressed *while* on a ladder. And a player should never move up a ladder if they're already at the very top!

```
                        chapter05/src/entities/_Entity.coffee (excerpt)

yo += @speed if keys.down and @onLadder
yo -= @speed if keys.up and @onLadder and not @onTopOfLadder
```

As you can see, ladders are easy enough to implement, but they present some tricky edge cases. Indeed, the first pass of the Professor's ladder code was much simpler, with none of the `onTopOfLadder` nonsense, or snapping—but the results were far less satisfying when playing.

Collecting

Things are really shaping up now, but the game still lacks a goal … it's just running around some platforms and ladders. The point of the game is for the Professor to reclaim his particle research from around his laboratory, so let's make the research particles collectible! We've already seen how to make a block climbable, so fortunately there's little that's new here.

In the `Block` base class, we'll add yet another property under `climbable` called `touchable`. Touchable things can be touched! Depending on who touches it, we can perform different actions; in this case, if the Professor touches a treasure, he'll collect it:

```
                          chapter05/src/blocks/_Block.coffee (excerpt)

class Block
  touchable: false
```

`touchable` is `false` for all blocks, except for our `Treasure` (at the moment). In addition, we'll add a flag to indicate if the block has been collected by the player:

```
                        chapter05/src/blocks/_Treasure.coffee (excerpt)

class Treasure extends Block
  touchable: true
  collected: false
```

Testing Class Types

To decide if an entity is touching a `touchable` block, we do exactly what we did for `climbables`. In the `Entity` class, we check `nearBlocks` to see if we're interested in any of the surrounding blocks. If so, we call the block's `touch` method (passing it the entity that touched it):

chapter05/src/entities/_Entity.coffee *(excerpt)*

```
# Collect any touchables
block.touch @ for block in nearBlocks when block.touchable
```

This, of course, implies that the block has a `touch` method, which we'll need to add to the `Treasure` class:

chapter05/src/blocks/Treasure.coffee *(excerpt)*

```
touch: (entity) -> @collected = true
```

Hmmm ... but now we have a problem. Currently, any entity is able to collect a `Treasure` block that it `touches`. But as we all know, ninjas are unable to pick up items—only the Professor can. So we have to check that the entity touching the block is the Professor. To do this, we use the `constructor` property that CoffeeScript exposes to us:

chapter05/src/entities/_Entity.coffee *(excerpt)*

```
touch: (entity) ->
  @collected = true if entity.constructor is Player
```

This works because the `constructor` property on a class instance *is the class itself*. So to test for ninjas, you'd check if it's the `Ninja` class: `if entity.constructor is Ninja`.

Now that we can trust it's the Professor picking up the treasure, we can remove it from the level. The `Treasure` block's `update` method needs a bit more information than our other blocks now. Previously, all blocks were self-contained, but the treasure needs to interact with the level, so we'll change the `Level` code that updates all blocks to add in this extra information:

chapter05/src/levels/Level.coffee *(excerpt)*

```
update: ->
  # Update the level blocks
  for row, y in @map
    for block, x in row
      block.update x, y, @
```

We're changing very little here—just passing in the additional x, y, and level information to each block. Because it's unnecessary for most blocks to interact directly with the level, they'll simply ignore those parameters. But our treasure needs it:

chapter05/src/blocks/Treasure.coffee *(excerpt)*

```
update: (x, y, level) ->
  @yOff +=  Math.PI / 24
  if @collected
    level.removeBlock x, y, @
```

The Level code has some interesting tasks to do if some treasure is collected. It replaces the Treasure block with an empty block (removing the treasure from the game), and, more importantly, it decrements its internal treasures count:

chapter05/src/levels/Level.coffee *(excerpt)*

```
removeBlock: (x, y, block) ->
  @map[y][x] = new Block()
  if block.constructor is Treasure
    if --@treasures == 0
      alert "Level Complete!"
      @game.reset()
```

As Figure 5.4 shows, if the count is 0, the level is finished!

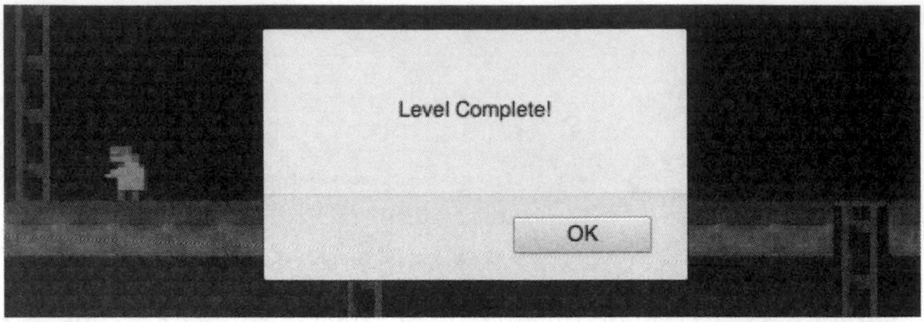

Figure 5.4. Doing your level best

Now the Professor has a job to do! We only have one level, so "Level Complete" in this instance means "Game Over." But for now, that's awesome.

Collision

The ninjas have been receiving a fairly raw deal up to now: they're unable to pick things up, and they can't even move. Let's at least give them one impressive power: the ability to kill the Professor instantly upon contact! At the bottom of the level's `update` method, after updating the ninjas, we add the following comprehension to test collisions between the Professor and the ninjas:

chapter05/src/levels/Level.coffee *(excerpt)*

```
@player.update()
@checkCollision @game.player, ninjas for ninjas in @ninjas
```

The `checkCollision` function will compare the bounding box of two entities. A **bounding box** is the rectangle made up from the four corner points of an entity. If two bounding boxes overlap, there's a collision, as seen in Figure 5.5.

Figure 5.5. Bounding boxes collide

In the first frame, a ninja is plummeting towards the Professor, but so far, the Professor is okay. In the second frame, however, the bounding boxes overlap—and we all know that overlapping a ninja is bad for your health:

chapter05/src/levels/Level.coffee *(excerpt)*

```
checkCollision: (p, b) ->
  if p.x + p.w >= b.x and
  p.x <= b.x + b.w and
  p.y + p.h >= b.y and
  p.y <= b.y + b.h
    alert "You are dead."
    @game.reset()
```

If you draw the points out on a piece of paper, you'll see that our test makes sense. The player's right edge must be more than the entity's left edge, and its left edge must be less than the entity's right edge; similarly for the top and bottom edge. This kind of test is called an **Axis-Aligned Bounding Box (AABB)** test. It's nice and easy to implement, and works great for any rectangular-ish objects (which you'll find most characters are!).

 Mad Skillz

Because AABB tests use the extreme edges of the entity, collisions can sometimes feel too sensitive. A common technique that fixes this is using a bounding box that's smaller than the entity. It can lead to some false negatives, but will make the player feel more adept at skillfully dodging a ninja!

Ninja AI

Our ninjas are now lethal, but they're far from stealthy. They just stand there being slightly dangerous like a pointy cactus might. To transform our cacti into formidable foes, we have to add some movement logic, which we'll loosely label **Artificial Intelligence**. Rather than an amazing feat of complex machine learning, our AI will be a series of simple rules that make it *look* like the ninja has a motive.

The motive is to seek out the Professor. The two modes to enact the motive are CRUISING and HUNTING. The ninja will start in CRUISING mode that works as follows:

1. Choose a direction to move: left, right, or idle.

2. Move in that direction for a random amount of time.

3. After the time is up, choose again.

Okay, that's hardly formidable so far—they just run around randomly. While cruising, there are two ways a ninja can change modes to HUNTING:

- if the ninja is on the same horizontal plane as the Professor (because the ninja can "see" him)

- when the ninja is touching a ladder randomly (sometimes the ninja will climb or descend to try to find the Professor)

In HUNTING mode, the ninja becomes obsessed with stalking the Professor and will try to move towards him by:

- moving left or right if they're on the same horizontal plane
- moving up or down if they're on a ladder
- going back to CRUISING mode if neither of these are true

In order for the ninja to chase the the player, we need to pass a reference to the Player in the constructor. A well-encapsulated approach would be to pass the game object reference when creating a Level, and then pass the @game.player object to each Ninja as we create them. To make things easier for the Professor, let's also make the ninjas move a little slower:

```
                                    chapter05/src/entities/Ninja.coffee (excerpt)

class Ninja extends Entity
  constructor: (level, x, y, @player) -> super level, x, y
  speed: 3
```

We'll create a simple **state machine** to implement the rules, and add two properties to the Ninja: state and subState. These will be simple strings that we'll use to identify where we are in the rules:

chapter05/src/entities/Ninja.coffee *(excerpt)*

```coffee
class Ninja extends Entity
  state: "CRUISING"
  subState: "IDLE"
  ⋮
```

We'll initialize the Ninja to CRUISING mode, and heading in the direction IDLE—so, just standing around. We also need a couple of functions for dealing with our different AI modes. They'll work the same: we'll give the current player position (px and py), they'll perform some logic, then pass back the x and y numbers to move as an array:

chapter05/src/entities/Ninja.coffee *(excerpt)*

```coffee
cruise: (px, py) ->
  x = y = 0
  # Do cruising logic
  [x, y]
hunt: (px, py) ->
  x = y = 0
  # Do hunting logic
  [x, y]
```

The amounts that come back from the AI logic are then fed into the entity's move function during an update. Notice the difference between the Professor and the ninjas? The Professor gets his x and y figuress directly from the user's keyboard actions, but the ninjas get it from our AI functions.

Destructured Assignment 2: Objects

Before we can do any AI calculations, we need to grab the Professor's current location and call the correct AI function. If the ninja is falling, then we don't want it to do anything (except fall), so we set the x and y move amounts to zero. Otherwise, we get the amounts from the corresponding functions and feed them into move:

chapter05/src/entities/Ninja.coffee *(excerpt)*

```coffee
update: ->
  [xo, yo] = if @falling then [0, 0] else
    {x: px, y: py} = @player
    switch @state
```

```
    when "CRUISING" then @cruise px, py
    when "HUNTING" then @hunt px, py

  @move xo, yo
```

That's a pretty dense bit of code for a single expression. The output of the expression is always an array of two values. The output comes either directly if the player is falling, or from the functions executed inside the `switch` statement. It's then destructured into the `xo` and `yo` variables, which we can pass to `move`.

But what is that line buried in the middle: `{x: px, y: py} = @player`? It's another example of destructured assignment but this time applied to objects!

One nicety is that if you want to destruct properties to variables *with the same name*, you don't even have to explicitly name them. So, if we wanted to assign the player's locations to variables named `x` and `y` (which is what they are called on the object), instead of this:

```
{x:x, y:y} = @player
```

… we could just write this:

```
{x, y} = @player
```

 Dig Deep

You can go deeper than a single level when pattern matching on objects. For example, we can easily pull information about the player from our `level` object:

```
{player: {speed, dir}} = level
console.log speed, dir // 4, "LEFT"
```

Just like destructuring arrays, destructuring objects helps eliminate a lot of boilerplate code and temporary variables—resulting in more beautiful code.

Adding the AI Rules into the Code

Converting our written AI rules to code is fairly straightforward. We start with our CRUISING code—depending on our substate, we either move left or right (or neither if the ninja is IDLE):

```
chapter05/src/entities/Ninja.coffee (excerpt)

# Do cruising logic
switch @subState
  when "RIGHT"
    x += @speed
    @dir = "RIGHT"
  when "LEFT"
    x -= @speed
    @dir = "LEFT"
```

Now we need a way to choose a new direction. We'll add a time: 0 property to the top of the Ninja class. This will be used to flag that it's time to change the strategy:

```
chapter05/src/entities/Ninja.coffee (excerpt)

time: 0
⋮
cruise: (px, py) ->
  ⋮
  if --@time < 0
    newMove = utils.rand 5
    @time = utils.rand 20, 40;
    @subState = switch newMove
      when 0, 1 then "LEFT"
      when 2, 3 then "RIGHT"
      else "IDLE"
```

Using the utils.rand utility method that you wrote as an exercise under Feeling adventurous? in Chapter 2, which is now in **chapter05/src/_utils.coffee**, we pick a number between 0 and 4. We weight the output to choose the new direction (there's a 2/5 chance of moving left or right, but only a 1/5 chance of being idle). We also assign a random time of between 20 and 40 ticks to move in the new direction. That's all we need for crazy ninjas!

But we want more—we need them to hunt down the Professor. If they start touching a ladder (that is, they are onLadder but not wasOnLadder), there's a random chance to switch to HUNTING mode:

chapter05/src/entities/Ninja.coffee *(excerpt)*

```
# Just touched a ladder
if @onLadder and not @wasOnLadder
  @state = "HUNTING" if Math.random() < 0.5
```

And if they can see the Professor directly, the hunt is definitely on!

chapter05/src/entities/Ninja.coffee *(excerpt)*

```
# Spotted the player… run at them!
@state = "HUNTING" if py == @y
```

Our HUNTING logic is simple enough. If we can see our target or we're standing on top of a ladder, we start moving in the direction of the Professor:

chapter05/src/entities/Ninja.coffee *(excerpt)*

```
# Do hunting logic
if py is @y or @onTopOfLadder
  if px > @x
    x += @speed
    @dir = "RIGHT"
  else
    x -= @speed
    @dir = "LEFT"
```

If the Professor's x is less than our x, we move left; otherwise, right:

chapter05/src/entities/Ninja.coffee *(excerpt)*

```
else if @onLadder
  y -= @speed if not @onTopOfLadder and py < @y
  y += @speed if py > @y
```

If we're on a ladder, we do the same as left and right, but in the y direction. Now the ninjas know how to climb!

```
else
  @state = "CRUISING"
  @subState = "LEFT"
```

The last possibility is that the player is out of view, in which case we switch back to CRUISING mode. It's quite amazing to see such simple rules give the appearance of a motive. Sure, they may not be the smartest ninjas on the block, but they make worthy opponents for the Professor, and making them smarter is just a matter of adding some new rules!

Power to the Professor

The day is wearing on, and you're starting to feel the pain. Your fingers are sore and you haven't stood up for the past three hours. The game is now in an acceptable working state, yet still you feel unfulfilled. The Professor lacks any kind of special powers. He *has* to be able to dig and build, otherwise he's technically not our Professor. You summon up your remaining strength for the last push …

Digging Holes

The Professor will be able to dig holes in platforms in order to create a sneaky escape route for himself, or to create a trap that averts a chasing ninja. Both digging and building involves meddling with the underlying map structure of our level. Digging will make a solid block unsolid, and vice versa. Both actions are temporary, and the results will be undone after a short delay.

We'll begin by modifying the Player. It needs a new property called lastDig that defaults to the current time (utils.now())—the last time the player dug a hole. This is used to prevent a player digging too quickly.

Digging will be triggered when the user hits the fire button (we'll use the space bar). This is handled near the other input checks inside update:

```
@dig() if keys.space

@move xo, yo
```

The `dig` method handles the timing we talked about (you can only dig once every 6,000 milliseconds) and after a dig has occurred, the `lastDig` time is set to now.

chapter05/src/entities/Player.coffee (excerpt)

```coffee
dig: ->
  return if utils.now() - @lastDig < (6 * 1000) # 6 seconds

  @level.digAt @dir, @x, @y
  @lastDig = utils.now()
```

The line in the middle does all the real work, however. It calls a new `digAt` method on the level class, passing the player's `direction`, x and y:

chapter05/src/levels/Level.coffee (excerpt)

```coffee
digAt: (dir, x, y) ->
  [xb, yb] = @getBlockIndex x, y

  xb = xb + if dir == "RIGHT" then 1 else -1
  return if yb + 1 > @h or xb < 0 or xb > @w - 1
  block = @map[yb + 1][xb]

  # Dig the block!
```

First, we retrieve the block's *x* and *y* indexes from the given player coordinate. Next, we check if the block in front or behind the player (depending on their direction) is inside the map. If it is, we know what the Professor is trying to dig.

As it stands, no blocks currently know how to be dug. The `Dirt` block is the only diggable element in the game, so we have to enable it to be dug. Add a `digTime` property and set it to `80`. This will indicate how long the hole will be on screen:

chapter05/src/blocks/Dirt.coffee (excerpt)

```coffee
digIt: ->
  @digTime = 80
  @solid = false
```

When the block's `digIt` method is called, the `digTime` is initialized and the block becomes unsolid, so our entities will pass right through it! We don't want that to be permanent, though, so we change it back in our `update` method:

chapter05/src/blocks/Dirt.coffee *(excerpt)*

```
update: ->
  @solid = true if --@digTime is 50
```

The block becomes solid again part way through the digTime countdown. This is because we want to fade the block in as it's becoming solid, but without waiting for the entire fade animation to occur before our entities can walk on it again. To do the fade, we temporarily modify the drawing context's globalAlpha property to a level that's a function of the current digTime:

chapter05/src/blocks/Dirt.coffee *(excerpt)*

```
render: (gfx, x, y) ->
  oldAlpha = gfx.ctx.globalAlpha
  gfx.ctx.globalAlpha = 1 - @digTime / 80
  gfx.drawSprite 4, 1, x, y
  gfx.ctx.globalAlpha = oldAlpha
```

When we dig, the block will become invisible, then slowly fade back in. All that's left to do is call the digIt function on a block (if it has one) to start the process. We do this at the end of the level's digAt function:

chapter05/src/levels/Level.coffee *(excerpt)*

```
# Dig the block!
block.digIt() if block.digIt?
```

Any block can implement the digIt function if it needs to be diggable.

Building Blocks

In our game, building is similar to digging, but there are a few important differences. You can dig any block that implements a digIt method, but you can only build on an empty block. The empty block is replaced with a completely new block. This block will be called Gravel, and we'll put it in **blocks/Gravel.coffee**:

chapter05/src/blocks/Gravel.coffee *(excerpt)*

```
class Gravel extends Block
  solid: true
  digTime: 100
```

```
update: (x, y, level) ->
  if --@digTime < 0
    level.removeBlock x, y, @

render: (gfx, x, y) ->
  oldAlpha = gfx.ctx.globalAlpha
  gfx.ctx.globalAlpha = @digTime / 50
  gfx.drawSprite 4, 2, x, y
  gfx.ctx.globalAlpha = oldAlpha
```

The `Gravel` class is similar to the `Dirt` class—except that when the block has existed for long enough (once our timer is down to 0), the block actually removes itself from the map, just as the `Treasure` block did.

To create a new block, we add just a single line to the end of the level's `digAt` method (below the `block.digIt()` call):

chapter05/src/levels/Level.coffee *(excerpt)*

```
# Building
@map[yb + 1][xb] = new Gravel() if block.constructor is Block
```

If the block the Professor is trying to dig is actually empty (that is, it's a `Block`), we create a new instance of `Gravel` and put it in the map.

Digging allows the Professor to make sneaky getaways from the ninjas, and building lets him reach otherwise inaccessible platforms and areas. Using these two game mechanics, we can now easily make some puzzle-like levels where the player has to carefully consider and use the Professor's powers to reach the treasure.

Set for Life

Holy cow. A game. Today, we've been to hell and back—but the results have been worth it. The base we've crafted over the previous chapters has proven to be powerful indeed. And adding each new feature was (relatively) easy.

The remaining team members huddle around your laptop, running the game through its paces and eagerly barking ideas of features for you to add. You're not listening, though; instead, you're enjoying a well-earned powernap.

CoffeeScript and HTML5 FX

You sit at the local café like a Zen master. Part of your team has abandoned the project; the remaining members squabble with each other, unconvinced that a fully working game can be hewn from the prototype you've produced thus far. You, however, are free from doubt. The path before you illuminates itself, bathed in a sea of elegant CoffeeScript: scrolling platforms, sound effects, animations, particle effects, game screens, and dialogs. CoffeeScript has become the path of least resistance between your brain and Professor Digman-Rünner.

HTML-ifying things

Day 1 of the "7-day HTML5 Game Jam-a-Thon Challenge (TM)" seems like a happy, hazy memory. You've changed a lot since those simpler times, and you know now is your last chance to steer the team back on track. They've lost faith in the game, so you need to really impress them to restore hope. It's at that very moment it hits you: so far we've all but ignored the fact we're working with web technologies. We have a utility belt of tools and techniques that can easily be employed both inside and on top of our current game.

Using jQuery

jQuery is a (some would say *the*) DOM and Ajax library for facilitating client-side manipulation of web pages: adding event handlers, adding classes and styles, creating elements and updating existing elements—all with impressive cross-browser support. Having just recently read an excellent book on the subject (*ahem jQuery Novice to Ninja*[1] *ahem*) you decide that the terseness of jQuery nicely matches CoffeeScript's, and so head over to http://www.jquery.com/ to download it.

To include jQuery in your CoffeeScript project, you need to install some dependencies, configure your package management system to, wait, what? No! We simply want to use jQuery (which is just JavaScript) in our CoffeeScript project, which is also just JavaScript! To set up any third-party libraries, dump them into your project (we'll use the **/vendor** folder) and include them in your HTML pages as usual:

chapter06/index.html *(excerpt)*

```
<script src="vendor/jquery-1.8.2.min.js"></script>
```

Nothing special is required to use third-party libraries, but CoffeeScript's elegance does tend to make working with them more fun. We'll change how we select the main game `canvas` element, in the `init` method of **gfx.coffee**, going from this:

```
canvas = document.querySelector("#game")
```

... to this:

chapter06/src/gfx.coffee *(excerpt)*

```
canvas = $("#game")[0]
```

You can see what we mean when we say jQuery is concise! Astute CoffeeScripters might note that we could equally use:

```
canvas = $ "#game" [0]
```

... omitting the parentheses. And indeed they'd be right: the `$` function is an alias to the `jQuery` function, and function calls in CoffeeScript don't need parentheses

---

[1] http://www.sitepoint.com/books/jquery2/

for parameters. However, it looks weird with the dollar sign floating by itself, and more importantly, it can lead to issues when we use one of jQuery's coolest features: function chaining. For a (contrived) example of chained function calls, here's how we'd add a new CSS class to the `canvas` element and make it disappear:

```
$("#game").addClass("screen").hide()
```

When we chain calls like this we typically have to leave the parentheses around the parameters so that CoffeeScript associates them correctly (see the section called "Function Gotchas" in Chapter 3).

We can use some more jQuery help in adding event handlers. This is a common source of cross-browser headaches, so we might as well take them out of the equation. In the **keys.coffee** file, we'll update our handcrafted efforts from this:

```
document.addEventListener "keydown", (e) ->
  keys.trigger e.keyCode, true
,false

document.addEventListener "keyup", (e) ->
  keys.trigger e.keyCode, false
,false
```

… over to jQuery's quite delightful shortcuts:

chapter06/src/keys.coffee *(excerpt)*

```
$(document).keydown (e) -> keys.trigger e.keyCode, true
$(document).keyup (e) -> keys.trigger e.keyCode, false
```

Do I need to use jQuery?

Our game is using a lot of HTML5 features that will only run in modern browsers. We can be quite confident that any browser that supports our game will also support the `addEventListener` and `querySelector` native methods correctly. This means you don't *have* to use jQuery—it's a nice library, but as browsers become better they start to fill in the holes that jQuery was written to patch!

Function Binding

There's one aspect that feels a bit strange with our event handlers, though. In the handler function, we have to reference the global `keys` object directly. It's because the scope of `this` (or its alias, `@`) *inside* the function has changed (thanks to JavaScript's scoping rules, `this` would refer to the global window object rather than our custom `keys` object). Similarly, our call to `setTimeout` in **game.coffee** refers to the global `game` object. A common method to circumvent this issue and retain the calling scope is to keep a reference to the outside scope in a closure:

```
self = @
setTimeout (-> self.tick()), 33
```

A **closure** encloses the execution environment of an outside scope with that of an internal scope; in the aforementioned example, the variable `self` is not defined in the event handler's context, but it *can* be found when JavaScript looks up its chain of scopes. Now we have a way of capturing a different value of `this`!

Keeping the scope in this way is sometimes called **function binding**, and is so common that CoffeeScript supplies a nice wrapper to take care of the plumbing for us. To use function binding in CoffeeScript, we utilize the "fat arrow" syntax:

chapter06/src/game.coffee *(excerpt)*

```
setTimeout (=> @tick()), 33
```

Notice that the scope *inside* the function handler is now the same as the scope in the calling function, namely our `game` object. Additionally, we have now banished the unsightly `self = this`.

One factor to be careful of, however, is that now we've changed the scope, the internal meaning of `this` has changed. In jQuery, for example, `this` usually refers to the DOM object/s that you've selected (which is very convenient). By using fat arrow syntax, we mess around with that, and therefore lose the reference. If we need to retrieve the object, it's actually passed as the `target` property on the event parameter:

```
$(document).keydown (e) => theDocument = e.target
```

When we need the original element, the jQuery code becomes more hideous. Hmmm, looks like we have a trade-off. It can be unclear when to use normal functions and when to use bound functions. Generally, if the code inside the function deals primarily with the calling code, use fat arrows; otherwise, stick to basic functions.

Closure Wrapper, with do

Function binding is great for event handlers, but if your goal is just to close over a variable (say, inside a loop), you can use CoffeeScript's do keyword. This wraps your code inside a function:

```
for url in urls
  do (url) ->
    $.ajax url,
      success: -> console.log url
```

Without the do wrapper, the `console.log` line would print the incorrect URL; by the time it executed, the `for` loop would have completed, and the value would be the last URL in the list.

CSS Effects

Creating games on the Web has some serious perils: HTML5 is still in its infancy, and we face constantly morphing browser implementations. New features are introduced on what seems like a weekly basis, and they change rapidly. Thankfully, the basics are relatively set in stone, though it's easy to forget they're there when swimming in the pool of awesome new HTML additions.

Take our game, for example. We've created our own complete rendering system for drawing pixels on the screen using the canvas element. One very interesting aspect of the canvas element is that it's just a DOM element (for instance, we can style it with CSS, just as we can with any DOM element!). This is an easy and cheap (cheap as in CPU cycles) way to add a bit of polish to our game without having to get our hands dirty in the Canvas API.

Styling Your Canvas

The quickest win we can look at is styling the canvas element itself. We're already rendering the background via a simple CSS property, but CSS3 gives us some super-cool features that can be used to add effects—effects that people playing the game will assume are just part of our rendering engine.

As an example, let's add a vignette to the entire surface. A vignette is the name of the effect that's employed heavily on hipster photo apps. With CSS3, we can add multiple backgrounds to an element by separating them with commas; so in addition to our brick background, we'll add a radial gradient to give a dark, ominous feeling to the action (replace `webkit` with other browser prefixes as necessary):

chapter06/css/main.css (excerpt)

```
#game {
  background:
    -webkit-radial-gradient(
      rgba(0, 0, 0, 0.0) 25%,
      rgba(0, 0, 0, 0.7)),
    url(resources/bg.png);
```

As CSS evolves, the power it brings is enormous, and with CSS filters on the horizon,[2] it looks even more promising. Applying CSS directly to our game is fairly wacky … some might even say "hacky." But game dev history is chock-full of these kinds of hacks used for impressive results.

Cheap Parallax Effect

Applying CSS to an element is a nice way to add a static effect, but we're making games here … static is no fun, everything needs to be dynamic! Of course, web pages are no stranger to dynamic elements, and, again, our game canvas is no exception. We can update CSS properties from inside the game, to create effects that would be a lot tougher to do in straight Canvas API code.

We'll demonstrate this with an effect that is a bit more dramatic: parallax scrolling. **Parallax scrolling** is the name of the effect where layers that are further in the background move more slowly than layers in the foreground. Our foreground is not scrolling at all, so our parallax effect will be a kind of weird "inverse parallax" for now (in a second we'll look at moving the foreground too).

---

[2] https://dvcs.w3.org/hg/FXTF/raw-file/tip/filters/index.html

Our plan is to link the background brick position to the player's location, using the `background-position` CSS property. In the **game.coffee** class, at the end of the rendering method, we add the following:

```
backX = 1 - (@player.x / gfx.w) * 100
backY = 1 - (@player.y / gfx.h) * 100
gfx.ctx.canvas.style.backgroundPosition = "#{backX}px #{backY}px"
```

We access the canvas's CSS styles via the `gfx.ctx.canvas.style` property. We set the `background-position` (marked as `backgroundPosition` in script) to the player's position as a percentage of the playing field. This gives an interesting scrolling effect—with no Canvas APIs needed!

These effects are only scratching the surface; you can go wild with combining technologies. Overlay styled `divs` or other regular DOM elements as layers, add CSS transition and animation effects, change class names dynamically—nothing is off limits. It's good fun to apply years of web-page development tricks directly to your game—and it can lead to some unusual and unexpected results.

Canvas Scrolling

There are some built-in tricks buried inside canvas too, and just as we took advantage of the inherent abilities of CSS to get some nice effects "on the cheap," we can do the same with canvas. So far, we've only been using canvas's rendering methods for drawing images, rectangles, and text, but the API also provides a few useful tools for manipulating the canvas object itself: `scale`, `rotate`, and `translate`.

These transformations work similarly to their CSS counterparts—stretching, rotating, and moving things around—but can be applied on an operation-by-operation basis. We need to take some care to accomplish this, because if we apply a transformation to a context, that transformation will be in effect for all future drawing operations. To avoid this, we should maintain a stack of transformations that we push and pop as required. To push and pop, we use the canvas methods `save` and `restore`. Here's how we'd apply it to our main game rendering in **game.coffee**:

chapter06/src/game.coffee (excerpt)

```
render: (gfx) ->
  gfx.ctx.save()
  // Do some tricks

  // Render the game
  @level.render gfx
  @player.render gfx
  gfx.ctx.restore()
```

To see why it's important to save and restore the context, imagine if we rotated the canvas by just 0.1 of a degree in the render function: c.rotate(0.1). You'd barely notice this, right? Try it out and see (by commenting out the save and restore lines). Woah, the game is spinning unplayably! The problem is that we aren't just rotating the canvas by 0.1 degrees, we're rotating it by 0.1 degrees *every frame*!

By calling restore, the canvas context is reset to the last save state, so we aren't compounding the rotation. To put this to use in our game, let's employ scale and translate to implement a cool scrolling effect. We'll scale up the canvas so everything is bigger (so we won't see the whole screen at once anymore). We then translate (move) the element so the player is in the center:

chapter06/src/game.coffee (excerpt)

```
// Do some tricks
gfx.ctx.scale 1.3, 1.3
leftEdge = 210
offx = if @player.x > leftEdge then -@player.x + leftEdge else 0
gfx.ctx.translate offx, -@player.y + 130
```

That. Is. Cool. We've squished in a lot of magic numbers there—what's going on? Well, the first step is straightforward: we scale up the canvas to 1.3 times its original size. We then figure out if the player is far enough away from the left edge of the level to require scrolling, and translate to the new position. Try messing around with the magic numbers to understand how the centering works.

Audio and Sound Effects

Audio has been the neglected, unloved, and largely unsupported cousin of the Web. Until recently, the state-of-the-art was dinky MIDI files, or Flash-based players. But the tide is turning! The new Web Audio API specification[3] provides the means for playing multiple sound files, as well as playing sounds you generate in code. Of course, not all browsers support all aspects of the Web Audio API specification, but at least there has been progress.

Acquiring suitable sounds for your game used to be a challenge. You could head out with a microphone and make field recordings, buy sample CDs, scour Freesound[4] for suitable noises, or lose a few days stuck inside audio synthesizers and digital signal processors. All these solutions are time-consuming and laborious, especially when our game jam schedule allows one hour for everything sound-related.

Thankfully, there's a standard go-to answer for game-jam sounds: sfxr[5] by Tomas Petterson. sfxr is a synthesizer specially designed to make random 8-bit effects for sounds like power-ups, explosions, character deaths, and other special effects. It's super easy to use and you can quickly craft a suite of sounds that match the ambience of your (8-bit) game.

Once we have our sounds, we create a new CoffeeScript file called **sound.coffee**, where we'll initialize the sounds and supply a convenient way to trigger them (if you don't want to make your own, sound files are provided to you in **resources/**):

chapter06/src/sound.coffee

```coffee
sound =
  audio: {}
  list:
    "dig": "dig.wav"
    "fall": "falling.wav"
    "particle": "particle.wav"
    "dead": "dead.wav"
  init: ->
    @audio[name] =
    new Audio "resources/#{url}" for name, url of @list
  play: (name) ->
    @audio[name]?.currentTime = 0;
    @audio[name]?.play()
sound.init()
```

---

[3] https://dvcs.w3.org/hg/audio/raw-file/tip/webaudio/specification.html

[4] http://www.freesound.org

[5] http://www.drpetter.se/project_sfxr.html

We have included four sounds to load: for digging, falling, dying, and finding a particle. The properties of the `sound` object are iterated over and loaded by creating a new instance of the HTML5 `audio` tag and passing the resource URL. The `play` method accepts the sound name and uses the native `currentTime` property to rewind the sound and then play it.

To play a sound in our game, decide where you want the triggering to happen. For example, in the `Treasure` class we remove the treasure block when the Professor collects it. This seems like the perfect place to play the magical "`particle`" sound:

chapter06/src/blocks/Treasure.coffee *(excerpt)*

```coffee
if @collected
  level.removeBlock x, y, @
  sound.play "particle"
```

The `sound` object above is quite naive: the `audio` tag is relatively new, and different browsers can only play certain file formats. Unfortunately this means for the moment we have to supply our audio resources in multiple formats, and do some feature detection in code; for example, `new Audio().canPlayType('audio/mpeg;')` will tell us if the browser thinks it knows how to play an MP3. In addition, we should ensure sounds have loaded fully before we try to play them. We can do this by listening for the `canplaythrough` event. To avoid this, we'll just use WAV files that everybody knows how to play. Finally, the `audio` element has a bunch of other methods and properties for controlling volume and such. The spec has more.[6]

Whatever you end up using, never make the mistake of leaving sound out of your game—even during a time-limited hackathon! Sound is very powerful. Good sounds can totally change the character and feel of your game, and help enormously in immersing a player in the action.

Animation

People might wonder why our game's set entirely on conveyor belts: everyone's just sliding around! We'll add some frames for when the Professor is falling, and provide a kind of walking animation—or, as we say in the biz, a walk cycle.

---

[6] http://www.w3.org/wiki/HTML/Elements/audio

Walk Animation

A **walk cycle** is the animation pattern that repeats over and over to give the illusion that our character is walking. A good walk cycle is difficult to perfect, as it consists of four to eight (sometimes more) individual animation frames that mimic human movement. Thankfully, we only want an 8-bit walk cycle. This will comprise two frames: legs up, legs down, fitting the style and aesthetics of our game. If we had an elaborate eight-frame walk cycle with lo-fi sprites, it would just feel wrong!

We can implement a two-frame cycle effortlessly, without needing to keep an internal count of which frame we're on. We'll use the ol' game dev trick of tying our animation frame to the current time. Add this helper to our `utils` object:

chapter06/src/_utils.coffee (excerpt)

```
counter: (max, speed = 100) -> Math.floor @now() / speed % max
```

The `counter` function takes a maximum value to count to, and a speed (default is 100ms). Dividing the current time by the speed results in the number of steps that have occurred since JavaScript's epoch: January 1, 1970. This only becomes useful when we take the modulus of those steps by the maximum value. Now we have a counter that counts to our maximum value, then resets—ad infinitum!

To use this for animation, we'll link a counter to the player's sprite. In the `Player.render` method, the sprite is defaulted to position 0 (the very first sprite in our sprite sheet), and if the user is holding down the left or right key, we make a counter from 0 to 1. We add this to the `drawSprite` call:

chapter06/src/entities/Player.coffee (excerpt)

```
fx = if @dir is "LEFT" then 2 else 0
fx += utils.counter 2 if keys.left or keys.right

gfx.drawSprite fx, 0, @x, @y
```

The result is the `fx` variable toggles between 0 and 1 every hundred milliseconds when the user is moving. The Professor runs! As will the ninjas:

chapter06/src/entities/Ninja.coffee *(excerpt)*

```
fx = if @dir is "LEFT" then 2 else 0
fx += utils.counter 2

gfx.drawSprite fx, 1, @x, @y
```

Using a counter tied to time is a quick-and-dirty way to animate sprites without worrying about state. It's a great trick to commit to memory for the next game jam!

Falling Animation

While we're in the `Player` render, we may as well add in the falling animation we drew for the Professor, way back at the beginning. The "falling" frames are on the second row of the **sprites.png** file. In the first cell, the Professor is facing right; in the second, he's facing left. Now we have to show different frames depending on whether he's falling or not:

chapter06/src/entities/Player.coffee *(excerpt)*

```
fy = fx = 0
isLeft = @dir is "LEFT"
if @falling
  fx = 1 if isLeft
  fy = 2
else
  fx = 2 if isLeft
  fx += utils.counter 2 if keys.left or keys.right

gfx.drawSprite fx, fy, @x, @y
```

Where to Go from Here

Although our time-based flip-book approach to animation is naive and limited, it does let us create an impressive array of movement with minimal artwork. If you find that your rendering code becomes an unmaintainable mess of `if` statements, you might want to beef it up—perhaps using a state machine like we did with the ninja AI!

Screens and Dialogs

Our game is going to scare the daylights out of users if, once loaded, it throws them straight into the deep end without warnings or instructions or anything. Though that sounds like it might be a cool idea for a horror/reality game, it's not the ambience we're striving for with Professor Digman-Rünner.

We want a title screen with some instructions on how to play, and an introduction to the Professor himself. We need a brief "Get ready!" screen before action commences, and, finally, we have to dispose of the ugly pop-up dialogs when the player dies or completes a level.

Adding Screens

First, we'll concentrate on adding the concept of a "screen" in our game. Screens will help us compose the flow throughout; for example, we could have one screen for the title page, one for options, and one for the gameplay. A screen takes up the entire view area, with only one screen running at a time.

Here's the idea behind our implementation of a screen: the main game object will hold a reference to the current screen, sending the update and render messages to this screen. This means it will no longer need references to levels and players—the game screen will now be responsible for that.

We'll create a simple Screen class to act as an interface for our subclasses. We'll call this _Screen.coffee and put it in the new screens directory:

```
                                              chapter06/src/screens/_Screen.coffee
class Screen
  constructor: ->
  update: ->
  render: (gfx) ->
```

This should be looking familiar by now! The game object will call the update and render functions for the current screen, so we need to specify these in the base class. Every screen in our game will then be a subclass of Screen. For example, let's create GameScreen.coffee; it's destined to become the new controller of the game:

chapter06/src/screens/GameScreen.coffee

```
class GameScreen extends Screen
```

We'll just leave it as a placeholder for now, and move on to the title screen.

Inserting a Title Screen

TitleScreen.coffee will have the admirable task of delivering the all-important first impression to the user:

chapter06/src/screens/TitleScreen.coffee *(excerpt)*

```
class TitleScreen extends Screen
  min: 20
  update: ->
    return if @min-- > 0
    game.screen = new GameScreen() if keys.space
```

The main purpose of the title screen is to display information, but we need to be able to dismiss the screen, too. We want to start the game when the player hits the space key. We check the keys object and if space is true, we replace the current screen (the title screen) with a new instance of the GameScreen. This seems fair enough, but what is the field called min that defaults to 20?

It's just a simple counter that prevents us from hitting the space key too quickly—if the title screen has been displayed for less than 20 ticks, we skip key processing. The reason for it is that the player might still be holding down the space key from when they died in the last game; without a delay, a new game would be immediately launched without the poor player having a chance to pause for a second.

Rendering the screen can be as simple or complex as you want. To test it out, we'll just render some static images and text, but you could include a counter to trigger animations, or sine effects (as we did with the treasure), or whatever you think will most entice your users to play:

chapter06/src/screens/TitleScreen.coffee *(excerpt)*

```
render: (gfx) ->
  c = gfx.ctx
```

```
gfx.clear()
c.drawImage gfx.title, 180, 10
# Some instructions
c.fillStyle = "#e0e0e0"
c.font = "14pt monospace"
gfx.drawSprite 5, 1, 480, 180
c.fillText "Collect all \"Pig's Boffin\" particles.",
  50, 210
c.fillText "Press space to start...", 50, 240
```

You'll also have to load the title image in the gfx.load method:

chapter06/src/gfx.coffee *(excerpt)*

```
@title = new Image()
@title.src = "resources/title.png"
```

Okay, the title screen is defined; now it's time to chop up our game object. We're going to strip out all the gameplay-related functionality from the game object and replace it with the screen functionality. First, we add the screen property to the game object with a default of null:

chapter06/src/game.coffee *(excerpt)*

```
@game =
  screen: null
```

In the game's reset method, we no longer initialize @screen and @player; instead, we specify the screen that we'd like to display when the game loads. In our case, that's the title screen:

chapter06/src/game.coffee *(excerpt)*

```
reset: ->
  @screen = new TitleScreen()
```

Finally, we have to update and render the screen. While we're in mid-refactor, we comment out the current code in the render and update methods, testing that our screens are working correctly. Then we'll replace it:

```
update: ->
  @screen.update()
render: ->
  @screen.render gfx
```

As we've done throughout, we simply pass the update and render messages along. The code that we commented out will be moved into the game screen soon, but let's test out the new title screen. If we run the new code, our familiar game is gone, but we do have a spiffy new title screen! Hitting the space key should launch the game screen … however, when we hit the space key, nothing happens.

Well, something does happen: the new GameScreen instance is created and the game object updates and renders it every frame, but we still need to implement the update and render methods.

The Game Screen

We still have to move all the existing game code from **game.coffee** into **GameScreen.coffee**. The game object becomes the controller of the highest-level activities: looping and passing messages to the correct screens. The GameScreen now takes charge of our players and levels. The stubbed-out class looks like this (the comments indicate the code is copied directly from the old game object):

```
class GameScreen extends Screen
  levelNumber: 0
  constructor: ->
    @player = new Player()
    @startLevel()
  setPlayer: (x, y, level) ->
    # Set the player to the correct level position
  update: ->
    # Update level, player, and check collisions
  startLevel: ->
    @level = new Level levels[@levelNumber], @
  levelComplete: ->
    if ++@levelNumber >= levels.length
      game.win()
    else
```

```
      @startLevel()
  render: (gfx) ->
    # Render the level
```

The `GameScreen` holds information that's relevant to the current game: loading the level, updating and rendering, and checking if the game has been completed. This is where you'd include details like "score" and "lives" if your game requires them.

Our game only has two screens: the title and the game. You'll probably want to add a few more; perhaps an "options" screen, or stand-alone "You win the game!" and "Game over" screens. Another option is to just pop up this information over the current screen. For that, we'll need dialog boxes …

Overlaying Dialogs

Dialogs work exactly the same as screens, except they're overlaid on the current screen, rather being a discrete unit of game workflow. We'll use dialogs to add a "Get ready!" message to the beginning of each level, as well as use them to replace the nasty pop-up boxes we've been using so far.

Just as for screens, let's make a new folder and call it **dialogs**. We'll create a base class containing our old friends `constructor`, `update`, and `render`:

chapter06/src/dialogs/_Dialog.coffee

```
class Dialog
  constructor: ->
  update: ->
  render: (gfx) ->
```

Now that our game object has been refactored, adding in dialogs is a cinch: we add a new property, `dialog`, and make sure we clear it in the `reset` function. Anytime the `dialog` property is set, the dialog will be displayed, and the action in the background will be paused:

chapter06/src/game.coffee *(excerpt)*

```
@game =
  dialog: null
  reset: ->
    @dialog = null
```

```
render: (gfx) ->
  @screen.render gfx
  @dialog.render gfx if @dialog

update: ->
  if @dialog?
    @dialog.update()
  else
    @screen.update()
```

Nothing scary here, though it's essential that the dialog is rendered after the screen (otherwise the dialog will be overwritten by the screen graphics), and that we only call the screen's `update` method if there is no dialog. Otherwise, the action would continue on in the background and ninjas would kill us—most unsportsman-like—while we were reading the dialog.

Our first dialog will be the "Get ready!" message when a level begins. Our level data structure has an additional field called `name`, which we'll pass into the dialog to display and store in the `level` field via the constructor:

chapter06/src/dialogs/LevelDialog.coffee

```
class LevelDialog extends Dialog
  time: 50
  constructor: (@level) ->
  update: ->
    if --@time == 0
      game.dialog = null
```

A dialog differs from a screen in that it has a countdown timer; when it expires, the countdown clears itself from the `game` object, and the menu is gone. For rendering, we'll draw a translucent rectangle and display the text in the box:

chapter06/src/dialogs/LevelDialog.coffee *(excerpt)*

```
render: (gfx) ->
  c = gfx.ctx
  c.save()
  c.translate 100, 150
  c.fillStyle = "hsla(205, 40%, 50%, 0.8)"
  c.fillRect 0, 0, 350, 200
```

```
c.fillStyle = "#e0e0e0"
c.fillText "#{ @level }", 50, 100
c.restore()
```

Streamlined Dialogs

Want to ensure that all your dialogs looked exactly the same? You could encapsulate the rectangle and text drawing into a separate function in the base class, and call the base `render` method before you do your dialog-specific rendering.

To display the dialog, we need to instantiate it and assign it to the game's `dialog` property at the point where we create a new level. Figure 6.1 shows the result:

chapter06/src/screens/GameScreen.coffee *(excerpt)*

```
@level = new Level levels[@levelNumber], @
game.dialog = new LevelDialog(levels[@levelNumber].name)
```

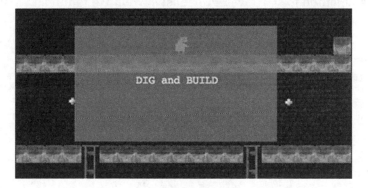

Figure 6.1. The level dialog gives users time to prepare

Adding further dialogs requires very little work: create the `Dialog` subclass with the dialog-specific drawing operations, then set it as the value of `game.dialog` when you want it to appear. To test this out, we'll implement a "Game over" dialog for when a player dies, in a file called **DeadDialog.coffee**:

chapter06/src/dialogs/DeadDialog.coffee

```coffee
class DeadDialog extends Dialog
  time: 100
  update: ->
    game.reset() if --@time == 0

  render: (gfx) ->
    c = gfx.ctx
    c.save()
    c.translate 100, 150
    c.fillStyle = "hsla(5, 40%, 50%, 0.8)"
    c.fillRect 0, 0, 350, 200

    c.fillStyle = "#e0e0e0"
    c.fillText "Ninjas have killed you!", 50, 100
    c.restore()
```

The "Game over" dialog runs for 100 ticks, displaying the unfortunate news of the Professor's untimely death. When the 100 ticks have passed, the dialog calls the game's reset method to start over. Previously, when we found a collision with a ninja, we would execute the code:

```coffee
alert "You are dead."
game.reset()
```

Now, we just have to create a dialog and it takes care of the rest (if you're yet to insert it, now is the perfect time to play the **dead.wav** sound effect):

chapter06/src/levels/Level.coffee *(excerpt)*

```coffee
sound.play "dead"
game.dialog = new DeadDialog()
```

It turns out, oddly enough, that winning is similar to dying for the Professor. Create a file called **WinDialog.coffee** with the same code, displaying a different message. And that's it. If you're feeling creative, you could (and should) create a completely separate screen for the final victory scene, so that the player feels all tingly when they successfully complete the vast challenges you've forced upon them.

Particles

You are fast running out of hours in the day, but you have the burning desire to add one more feature before you're done: a feature so powerful it can transform the dreariest of games into a eye-boggling visual feast … the particle effect! A **particle effect** is a collection of tiny visual pieces that each move and change separately, but work together to give the impression of smoke, fire, magic, or other abstract concepts. Abstract concepts! That's how powerful they are. For an example of a relatively feature-rich particle system, go have a look at Parcycle.[7]

A particle system can be as complex or simple as need be, and they're lots of fun to code. Each individual particle is given some specific properties, as well as some simple rules that evolve these properties. Individually they look … well, like nothing at all, really … but combined—that's when the magic happens.

A crazy super-high-res effect system will sit poorly with the lo-fi 8-bit aesthetic we've been cultivating thus far, so we need to be careful. The idea is to create a particle effect for when the Professor digs—but instead of the tiny gradient-filled particles of Parcycle, we'll use large flat rectangular particles.

Our system will comprise three parts: an individual particle, a controller to wrangle all the particles, and an object that specifies the initial properties and rules for our effect. We'll put all the components in a file named **Particle.coffee** in a **particles** folder. It commences with our final dig effect, which contains the following rules:

chapter06/src/particles/Particle.coffee *(excerpt)*

```
digParticles =
  life: 20
  num: 6
  size: [6, 4]
  xStart: [-2, 8]
  yStart: [-5, 0]
  xVelocity: [-1, 0]
  yVelocity: [-4, -1]
  acc: [0, 0.3]
  col:
```

---

[7] http://www.mrspeaker.net/dev/parcycle

```
h: 20
s: 60
l: 40
```

The whole effect will last for 20 ticks, and be made up of six individual particles each 6 pixels by 4 pixels in size (`life`, `num`, and `size` properties respectively). Each particle will start at a random *x* position between −2 and 8 pixels from the player's location, and its horizontal velocity will vary between −1 and 0. The *y* properties are specified in the same way. In each frame, acceleration is applied separately to the horizontal and vertical components of the particle's velocity. And finally, the particle will be set an HSL color value of (20, 60%, 40%).

Phew. That seems like a lot of properties—but particle systems can be far more complicated than this! The next step is to define the individual pieces. We'll make a class, `Particle`, that uses the rules from the options we defined:

chapter06/src/particles/Particle.coffee *(excerpt)*

```
class Particle
  constructor: (x, y, @opt) ->
    @a = 0.5
    @x = x + utils.rand @opt.xStart[0], @opt.xStart[1]
    @y = y + utils.rand @opt.yStart[0], @opt.yStart[1]
    @xVelocity = utils.rand @opt.xVelocity[0], @opt.xVelocity[1]
    @yVelocity = utils.rand @opt.yVelocity[0], @opt.yVelocity[1]
  update: ->
    @a -= 0.01
    @x += @xVelocity
    @y += @yVelocity
    @xVelocity += @opt.acc[0]
    @yVelocity += @opt.acc[1]
  render: (gfx) ->
    gfx.ctx.fillStyle =
    "hsla(#{@opt.col.h}, #{@opt.col.s}%, #{@opt.col.l}%, #{@a})"
    gfx.ctx.fillRect Math.floor(@x), Math.floor(@y), @opt.size[0],
    @opt.size[1]
```

Simple math is applied to each particle during each frame, to update its appearance and position. The `a` property is for the alpha value of the particle, which is set to fade over time (decreasing by 0.01 each frame). This could be implemented as a field if you wanted to vary it for other effects.

To wrangle a bunch of particles, we need a controller. The `Particles` class—as distinct from `Particle`—will take care of our collection of particles. When we start the effect, we can pass our options in, but we also use CoffeeScript's default parameters to employ the `digParticles` by default.

chapter06/src/particles/Particle.coffee *(excerpt)*

```coffee
class Particles
  constructor: (x, y, @opt = digParticles) ->
    @life = @opt.life
    @ps = (new Particle(x, y, @opt) for [0..@opt.num])

  update: ->
    p.update() for p in @ps
    @life-- > 0

  render: (gfx) -> p.render gfx for p in @ps
```

We use a nice little `for` comprehension to create the batch of particles, and then update and render them each frame. If the life of the particle system is over, we return `false` to indicate we're done processing this batch.

We want to create an instance of `Particles` every time the player digs or builds a block. This means that we need a way to wrangle the wrangler: we want a collection of a collection of particles! This is handled in the `Level` class.

First, a container is added as a property:

chapter06/src/levels/Level.coffee *(excerpt)*

```coffee
particles: []
```

... as well as a simple helper method for creating new effects:

chapter06/src/levels/Level.coffee *(excerpt)*

```coffee
addParticles: (x, y) ->
  @particles.push new Particles x, y
```

And finally, as we've typed a million times already, each element is given the update and render messages (we've put them at the very end of each method):

```
                                   chapter06/src/levels/Level.coffee (excerpt)

update: ->
  @particles = (p for p in @particles when p.update())

render: (gfx) ->
  p.render gfx for p in @particles
```

Notice that we're reassigning the `particles` array each frame using the filter keyword `when`. When a particle effect is complete and its `update` method returns `false`, it will be removed from the array (because the effect has finished).

To put the effect into the game, we have to call the `addParticle` helper, supplying the Professor's *x* and *y* positions. We do this at the end of the `digAt` function in **Level.coffee**, just before we play the dig sound!

```
                                   chapter06/src/levels/Level.coffee (excerpt)

@addParticles xb * gfx.tileW, (yb + 1) * gfx.tileH
sound.play "dig"
```

Look at those pretty dirt particles fly! Particle systems are extremely addictive, so you're encouraged to dig in and expand this simple system as much as you can, and add particles wherever possible: when the Professor is falling, when he lands, when the ninjas change direction, on the splash screen … everywhere!

Game Over

Holy cow. You lean back from your laptop and make two simultaneous realizations: one, you haven't taken a breather for the last few hours, so now's probably a good time to do that. And two, you've made a video game. A video game with heroes and villains, and animations, and dialogs, and scrolling, and sounds … You look over at the web guy and the artist. They're just twiddling their thumbs, reading Reddit.

It seems you ended up making the entire game by yourself. And as you put Professor Digman-Rünner through his final paces, you realize it's probably better this way.

Chapter

Epilogue

And on the Seventh Day ...

There's one remaining day in the "7-day HTML5 Game Jam-a-Thon Challenge (TM)," but frankly, you've decided it's unnecessary.

Six days ago, you made the insane decision to undertake the challenge with the notable handicap of never having used the language before, yet here you now stand with time on your hands. Working quickly and efficiently requires tools that let you express yourself clearly and tersely, and CoffeeScript fits that bill very nicely indeed.

Starting with the very basics, we powered through variable scoping, basic functions, and loops. We took these building blocks and applied them to mastering data structures and drawing items on the screen. Professor Digman-Rünner was born.

With the foundations laid, we dived into the juicy parts: list comprehensions, advanced function features, and destructured assignment. Like Frankenstein, we brought the game to life with the game loop and CoffeeScript's class system.

The spirit of CoffeeScript coursed through our veins, and we could move on to the true purpose of learning to code in *any* language: prying ideas out of our head and onto the screen. To this end, we added (with consummate ease) ninjas and collision detection, digging and building, ladders, scrolling, particles, animation—

Your remaining team members abruptly interrupt your flashback.

"Listen, we've been talking," they start. "And we know we dropped the ball for game jam … but we we want to make it up to you. Have a look at this concept art we did for a new game." The pixel artist hands you a sketch book. It contains a familiar face and the phrase:

Professor Digman-Rünner 2: Diggin' 'n' Runnin'.

"What do you think? We do all the art, you provide the coding magic?" They look at you with hope and excitement. You give a sigh, shrug, and say, "I guess I'll just have to brew up a fresh pot of CoffeeScript."

One coffee-based pun for the entire week. I think we can live with that.

Index

Hey ...

Thanks for buying this book. We really appreciate your support!

We'd like to think that you're now a "Friend of SitePoint," and so would like to invite you to our special "Friends of SitePoint" page.

Here you can SAVE up to 43% on a range of other super-cool SitePoint products.

Save over 40% with this link:

Link: 🌐 sitepoint.com/friends

Password: friends